Staging the *Amistad*

MODERN African Writing

from Ohio University Press
Laura T. Murphy and Ainehi Edoro, Series Editors

This series brings the best African writing to an international audience. These groundbreaking novels, memoirs, and other literary works showcase the most talented writers of the African continent. The series also features works of significant historical and literary value translated into English for the first time. Moderately priced, the books chosen for the series are well crafted, original, and ideally suited for African studies classes, world literature classes, or any reader looking for compelling voices of diverse African perspectives.

Welcome to Our Hillbrow
  A Novel of Postapartheid South Africa
  Phaswane Mpe
  ISBN: 978-0-8214-1962-5

Dog Eat Dog
  Niq Mhlongo
  ISBN: 978-0-8214-1994-6

After Tears
  Niq Mhlongo
  ISBN: 978-0-8214-1984-7

From Sleep Unbound
  Andrée Chedid
  ISBN: 978-0-8040-0837-2

On Black Sisters Street
  Chika Unigwe
  ISBN: 978-0-8214-1992-2

Paper Sons and Daughters
  Growing Up Chinese in South Africa
  Ufrieda Ho
  ISBN: 978-0-8214-2020-1

The Conscript
  A Novel of Libya's Anticolonial War
  Gebreyesus Hailu
  ISBN: 978-0-8214-2023-2

Thirteen Cents
  K. Sello Duiker
  ISBN: 978-0-8214-2036-2

Sacred River
  Syl Cheney-Coker
  ISBN: 978-0-8214-2056-0 (hardcover)
  978-0-8214-2137-6 (paperback)

491 Days: Prisoner Number 1323/69
  Winnie Madikizela-Mandela
  ISBN: 978-0-8214-2102-4 (hardcover)
  978-0-8214-2101-7 (paperback)

The Hairdresser of Harare
  Tendai Huchu
  ISBN: 978-0-8214-2162-8 (hardcover)
  978-0-8214-2163-5 (paperback)

Mrs. Shaw
  Mukoma Wa Ngugi
  ISBN: 978-0-8214-2143-7

The Maestro, the Magistrate &
    the Mathematician
  Tendai Huchu
  ISBN: 978-0-8214-2205-2 (hardcover)
  978-0-8214-2206-9 (paperback)

Tales of the Metric System
  Imraan Coovadia
  ISBN: 978-0-8214-2225-0 (hardcover)
  978-0-8214-2226-7 (paperback)

The Extinction of Menai
  Chuma Nwokolo
  ISBN: 978-0-8214-2298-4

The Wolf at Number 4
  Ayo Tamakloe-Garr
  ISBN: 978-0-8214-2354-7 (hardcover)
  978-0-8214-2355-4 (paperback)

Staging the Amistad
  Matthew J. Christensen, ed.
  ISBN 978-0-8214-2360-8 (hardcover)
  978-0-8214-2361-5 (paperback)

Staging the *AMISTAD*

THREE SIERRA LEONEAN PLAYS

Amistad Kata-Kata
by Charlie Haffner

The *Amistad* Revolt
(adapted from the novel *Echo of Lions*, by Barbara Chase-Riboud)
by Yulisa Amadu Maddy

The Broken Handcuff
by Raymond E. D. de'Souza George

Edited and introduced by **MATTHEW J. CHRISTENSEN**

OHIO UNIVERSITY PRESS   ATHENS

Ohio University Press, Athens, Ohio 45701
ohioswallow.com
© 2019 by Ohio University Press
All rights reserved

To obtain permission to quote, reprint, or otherwise reproduce or distribute material from Ohio University Press publications, please contact our rights and permissions department at (740) 593-1154 or (740) 593-4536 (fax).

Printed in the United States of America
Ohio University Press books are printed on acid-free paper ♾ ™

Cover art: Contemporary painting of the sailing vessel La Amistad off Culloden Point, Long Island, New York, 26 August 1839

29 28 27 26 25 24 23 22 21 20 19   5 4 3 2 1

Library of Congress Cataloging-in-Publication Data

Names: Christensen, Matthew J. (Matthew James), 1970- editor, writer of introduction.
Title: Staging the Amistad : three Sierra Leonean plays / edited and introduced by Matthew J. Christensen.
Description: Athens : Ohio University Press, [2019] | Includes bibliographical references.
Identifiers: LCCN 2019008904| ISBN 9780821423608 (hc : alk. paper) | ISBN 9780821423615 (pb : alk. paper)
Subjects: LCSH: Slaves--Sierra Leone--Drama. | Sierra Leonean drama (English)--20th century.
Classification: LCC PR9393.7 .S73 2019 | DDC 822/.9140809664--dc23
LC record available at https://lccn.loc.gov/2019008904

Contents

Introduction: Staging the *Amistad*   vii
MATTHEW J. CHRISTENSEN

Timeline   xxvii

Sengbe Pieh: A Ballad   1
CHARLIE HAFFNER

Amistad Kata-Kata   7
CHARLIE HAFFNER

The *Amistad* Revolt   61
(Adapted from the Novel *Echo of Lions*,
by Barbara Chase-Riboud)
YULISA AMADU MADDY

The Broken Handcuff   121
RAYMOND E. D. DE'SOUZA GEORGE

Acknowledgments   161

Notes   163

Suggested Reading   167

Introduction

Staging the *Amistad*

MATTHEW J. CHRISTENSEN

> Any black African artist who performs his art seriously, professionally and with sincere dedication to his people ought to use the past with the intention of opening up the future, as an invitation to action and a basis for hope. He must take part in the action and throw himself body and soul into the national struggle.
>
> —Yulisa Amadu Maddy (paraphrasing Frantz Fanon), "His Supreme Excellency's Guest at Bigyard"

INCLUDED HERE in print for the first time are historical dramas about the *Amistad* slave revolt by three of Sierra Leone's most influential playwrights of the latter decades of the twentieth century, Charlie Haffner, Yulisa Amadu Maddy, and Raymond E. D. de'Souza George. Prior to the initial public performance of the first of these plays, Haffner's *Amistad Kata-Kata*, in 1988, the 1839 shipboard slave rebellion and the return of its victors to their homes in what is modern-day Sierra Leone had remained an unrecognized chapter in the country's history. For the three playwrights, the events of the insurrection provided a new narrative for understanding Sierra Leone's past and for mobilizing the nation to work collectively toward a just and prosperous future. This renewed examination of Sierra Leonean history coincided with the near collapse of the great dream of political independence from British colonization. Fueling the drive for self-rule had been the expectation of political and economic equality on the world stage. In Sierra Leone, as in so many other parts of Africa and the formerly colonized world, the persistent structural inequities of global capitalism, the cynical capture of the state by venal kleptocrats, and the post–Cold War geopolitical realignments conspired to preempt the realization of these expectations. Sierra Leoneans suffered worse than most the results. The combined effects of global inequality, political self-dealing, and debilitating economic misery found their most horrific form in a decade-long civil war that began in 1991. The conflict took tens of thousands of lives and displaced 2.6 million people.[1] How Sierra Leoneans had let the dreams of freedom and equality slip from their grasp and how to reenergize them were not new topics for the country's writers, but they took on a new and more profound urgency in this period.

To explore these questions, Haffner, Maddy, and de'Souza George could have drawn on any number of uprisings, rebellions, and insurgencies in Sierra Leone's past, including the country's most famous, Bai Bureh's anticolonial war of 1898. In the events of the *Amistad* slave insurrection and its legal aftermath, however, the playwrights discovered especially rich material to examine historically and allegorically the discrepancy between the dreams of independence and its lived reality. The revolt took place off the Cuban coast in the early morning hours of July 2, 1839. Led by Sengbe Pieh (known also by his slave name Joseph Cinqué), fifty-three Africans broke their chains, took up a cache of cane knives, and commandeered the ship. Once liberated, the men and children, mostly Mende speakers, attempted to sail the schooner back to their home in the area of West Africa that is now southern and eastern Sierra Leone. Their initial freedom was short-lived. Unschooled in navigation, Sengbe Pieh, Grabeau, Burnah, and the other mutineers found themselves at the mercy of the Spaniards, Pedro Montes and Jose Ruiz, who sailed east by day but west and north by night, ensuring

Introduction: Staging the *Amistad*

that the *Amistad* never strayed far from North America. In late August, the schooner was seized anew by a U.S. naval vessel and transported to New London, Connecticut, where the Amistads, as the Africans came be known, were jailed on piracy charges and made the curious objects of a legal battle over the regulation of international commerce, national sovereignty, and the natural right to liberty. By its conclusion a year and a half later, with an unlikely victory for the Amistads in the U.S. Supreme Court, the drama involved no less than the Queen of Spain and U.S. presidents Martin Van Buren and John Quincy Adams. Theirs was not, nor would ever be, a completely unqualified triumph. Upon his long-awaited return to his village, Sengbe Pieh found his family and entire village had vanished, presumably victims of the slave trade. Moreover, neither he nor the other mutineers, nor any other inhabitant of Mendeland for that matter, would ever be able to escape fully the patronizing and paternalistic oversight of white Westerners. The Christian mission set up by the white Americans accompanying the *Amistad* mutineers would eventually blossom and later be turned over to the British-based United Brethren of Christ Church, which, in turn, paved the path for British colonization of what was to become Sierra Leone.

Like the anticolonial discourses of earlier Sierra Leonean and African writers, Haffner, de'Souza George, and Maddy seek to reinvigorate the promise of decolonization by narrating the *Amistad* history in ways that privilege the values of collective endeavor, the political agency of everyday Sierra Leoneans, Sierra Leone's power to shape world affairs, and, above all, liberty. Theirs are heroic tales of the oppressed and downtrodden asserting their rights in a world incapable of recognizing African dignity or sovereignty. The *Amistad* revolt proved doubly resonant in this regard because enslavement has featured more prominently in Sierra Leone's historical consciousness of itself than in most other West African nation-states. Capital city Freetown was founded in 1787 as a haven for freed slaves from the Americas and, after the abolition of the transatlantic slave trade in 1808, the city expanded with an influx of arrivals from the entire West African coast who had been liberated from illegal slave ships by

British patrols. Thus, for a country in which the meanings of liberty and equality remain shaped as much by the experience of the Atlantic-world slave economy as by the tyranny of colonization, the *Amistad* insurrection's narrative of capture, enslavement, Middle Passage, liberation, and return reenergizes the common account of Sierra Leone's origin and its status as a "province of freedom." Yet, at the same time, the playwrights, de'Souza George especially, also find in the *Amistad* narrative material for questioning how Sierra Leone, with all its promise at the time of independence from British colonialism in 1961, could have found itself so quickly engulfed in such a quagmire of misery. Unlike the vast majority of the liberated African Americans and West Africans (largely Yoruba) who originally settled Freetown, the *Amistad* revolt's protagonists and the slave-catchers who sold them into slavery hailed from communities that are part of modern-day Sierra Leone. The capture of the *Amistad* mutineers more than fifty years after Freetown's founding thus served as a powerful reminder that just outside Freetown's confines the Atlantic trade raged on. For as much as the plays celebrate the will to freedom emblematized by the *Amistad* rebels, they simultaneously highlight the pernicious social divisions and devaluation of individual life that made permissible the commodification and sale of Africans by other Africans during the era of the transatlantic trade and that were so apparent in Sierra Leone in the postindependence period when the three plays were written.

That the story of the *Amistad* rebellion found its home on the Sierra Leonean stage and that so many different playwrights would mine the narrative to rethink the country's past and future is not surprising. Lacking neither dramatic conflict nor narrative suspense in its account of despotism, heroic struggle, and courtroom sparring, the history makes for good theater. In fact, in 1839, only four days after the mutineers found themselves imprisoned in New Haven jail cells and long before any reliable information about what actually occurred was available, New York City's Bowery Theater staged a sensationalized "nautical drama" of "Piracy! Mutiny! & Murder!" titled "The Black Schooner, or the Pirate Slaver Armistad" [*sic*].[2] To this day, the rebellion remains a seductive topic for U.S. writers, artists, and performers.

Introduction: Staging the *Amistad*

Owen Davis in the 1930s and opera librettist Thulani Davis and filmmaker Steven Spielberg in the 1990s brought the mutiny to stage and screen. Poets Muriel Rukeyser, Robert Hayden, Kevin Young, and Elizabeth Alexander, novelist Barbara Chase-Riboud, and muralist Hale Woodruff have explored its themes of liberty and heroism. Even Herman Melville draws from the Amistads' mastery of the ship and its White commanders for its narrative conflict in his novella *Benito Cereno*. And this is just a short sampling. Apart from Spielberg's *Amistad* (1997), released nearly a decade after Charlie Haffner's *Amistad Kata-Kata* premiered, few of these works would have been available in Sierra Leone and none circulated outside small circles, but a similar recognition of the rebellion's historical and cultural import and its theatrical potential captured the country's playwrights. Perhaps even more importantly, in Sierra Leone the stage has served as a primary site for exploring political and social questions such as those provoked by the *Amistad* history. This is due in part to drama's disproportionate impact in a country with low literacy levels and a tiny population able to afford newspapers, books, or magazines. It is also a function of the country's dynamic oral storytelling cultures and ritual performance traditions. And, as in many other former British colonies worldwide, stage drama enjoyed a privileged status as both entertainment and social critique throughout much of the twentieth century.

Stage drama was first brought to England's colonies as a performative assertion of Britishness, and it was not uncommon to find elaborate theaters staging Elizabethan drama at the farthest-flung outposts of the empire. By the 1930s, Sierra Leoneans had begun to adapt, transform, and indigenize the theater with Krio-language translations of Shakespeare, for example, and with original scripts reflecting African realities.[3] Beginning in the late 1960s, Yulisa Amadu Maddy shifted Sierra Leonean drama away from manneristic plays about Freetown's high society to gritty realist narratives centered on the lives of petty thieves, street boys, and prostitutes who suffered firsthand the legacies of colonial racism and the hypocrisies of the social, political, and economic elite. Maddy's plays and his position as head of the drama department at Sierra Leone Radio ushered in a new generation of playwrights, including Charlie Haffner's and Raymond de'Souza George's mentor, Dele Charley, dedicated to exposing corruption and the abuses of power in the young nation-state.[4] If the colonial-era productions enabled white administrators and merchants to buttress their Britishness against what appeared to them as the heart of darkness (as well as, of course, to impart the so-called gift of their culture to the colonized), theater for Maddy's generation was critical in illuminating the threats to Sierra Leone-ness while simultaneously keeping alive the nationalist ideals that fueled the drive to independence. Because they drew attention to internal as well as external threats, their work did not go unpunished. In reaction to Maddy's play *Big Berrin* (1976), which takes aim at the excesses of Sierra Leone's political elite, President Siaka Stevens jailed Maddy, added dramatic works to the country's censorship act, and closed Freetown's largest and most popular venue.[5] These actions dampened political critique in the theater for nearly a decade, but Maddy's generation had firmly established theater as the dominant mode of cultural production and cultural critique—more so than the novel—and as the literary form for which the country's writers became internationally known. At the time Haffner began writing *Amistad Kata-Kata*, there remained, even in the face of government hostility, more than forty active drama companies in Freetown, a city with a population of only about one million.

Despite theater's popularity, producing a play in the 1980s about an 1839 slave revolt that took place in the Americas remained neither a risk-free proposition nor an obvious choice of topic. During the worst years of the government's clampdown on the arts, staging a play about armed insurrection was a likely ticket to jail. A few years prior to the premiere of *Amistad Kata-Kata*, President Siaka Stevens imprisoned a group of actors on charges of inciting violence after they attempted to stage a play about the nineteenth-century anticolonial leader Bai Bureh.[6] As a brash, novice playwright with dreams of transforming Sierra Leonean society, Charlie Haffner was nevertheless savvy enough to avoid the same fate. Although *Amistad Kata-Kata* neither lacks veiled critiques of contemporary Sierra Leonean society nor shies away from celebrating armed insurrection against tyrannical overlords, Haffner

Introduction: Staging the *Amistad*

made astute use of the new president Joseph Saidu Momoh's 1985 campaign platform, "Constructive Nationalism," to fashion his historical narrative as a tale of civic pride in which Sierra Leoneans take center stage in international affairs. *Amistad Kata-Kata* was thus all the more subversive for not proclaiming its subversiveness.[7] The bigger challenge, however, might have been that the revolt history was almost entirely unknown in the country. In various interviews and presentations, Haffner has described the deep skepticism of Sierra Leonean audiences who refused to believe that common villagers could have played so prominent a role on the global stage without the revolt having already become a central chapter in the country's historical narrative of itself.[8] For Haffner, as again for Raymond de'Souza George six years later, the skepticism was symptomatic of the very problems that he sought to address in the first place and would lead him to write a play that is as much about the necessity for a robust culture of public memory as it is about the *Amistad* rebellion itself.

Amistad Kata-Kata

Of the three plays included here, Haffner's *Amistad Kata-Kata* was the first one written and remains the only one to have been staged primarily in Sierra Leone. Born in 1953, Haffner was first introduced to the *Amistad* narrative as a student at Fourah Bay College, in Freetown, by the American anthropologist and historian Joseph Opala. A lively and dynamic lecturer with an unwavering belief that Sierra Leone lacked a set of shared symbols on which to build a national civic pride, Opala had started championing Sengbe Pieh as just such a symbolic figure about the same time Haffner enrolled in the college's Institute of African Studies. Opala was not the first to recognize the leading role Sierra Leoneans played in the revolt. Sierra Leonean historian Arthur Abraham had written about Sengbe Pieh previously. But Opala was perhaps the most vociferous. Inspired by Opala's lectures and his ideas about heroic nationalist symbols, Haffner wrote the first draft of *Amistad Kata-Kata* in 1986 as an assignment for Opala's course on national consciousness. He premiered the play with the Freetong Players, the theater troupe he founded for the purpose, two years later, in 1988, at the British Council auditorium in Freetown. The Freetong Players also recorded a popular narrative ballad, "Sengbe Pieh," included in this volume, that they and other groups performed in schools, lorry parks, markets, and just about anywhere they could find an audience. Almost single-handedly, *Amistad Kata-Kata* made the 1839 shipboard rebellion and Sengbe Pieh central figures in Sierra Leone's historical imaginary.

Amistad Kata-Kata unfolds as a relatively conventional nine-scene stage drama. The play is plot driven, featuring a chronological narrative that begins with Sengbe Pieh's capture, proceeds with the Amistads' sale in Havana and their shipboard uprising, and concludes with the U.S. Supreme Court trial. Its one departure from the historical record comes in the form of a frame narrative set in a Mende village in the 1980s in which a university student and his grandmother discuss the imperatives of historical memory. In its frame and core narratives, *Amistad Kata-Kata* privileges accessibility over aesthetic complexity, favors clear dialogue over stylized language, and keeps symbolism and metaphor to a minimum. Despite the seriousness of the topic, the play does not shy away from occasional humor. Its depiction of the would-be Cuban slave owners as woebegone subjects of the victorious *Amistad* rebels regularly generated laughs during the performances I viewed in Freetown in 1990 and 1991, as did depictions of Sengbe Pieh flustering his white American foes by demanding to be called by his Mende name. In terms of its staging, the play requires few props and no complicated lighting, sound, or other theatrical apparatus, its modest demands reflecting the conditions of the Sierra Leonean auditoriums, public parks, school lecture halls, and other informal venues available to the country's theater companies. While Haffner gives the play a Krio-language title that translates loosely as "Amistad Revolt," the play itself is in English.

Thematically, *Amistad Kata-Kata* aims for a similar transparency, returning repeatedly to a few key points. The play depicts the rebels as never anything less than the authors of their own lives even in the moments when freedom seemed most remote; it insists that cultural self-respect is the bulwark to withstanding the crushing forces of geopolitically dominant institutions such as the transatlantic slave trade

Introduction: Staging the *Amistad*

or the U.S. legal system; and it posits historical memory as a necessary foundation for civic well-being. This is not to say that *Amistad Kata-Kata* shies away from aesthetic or thematic nuance. In its interplay of oral and written historical practices, the play problematizes meanings of modernity, and in its employment of the multivalent trope of cannibalism, it situates the *Amistad* rebellion as just one, though uniquely emblematic, moment in the long history of suffering under the regimes of global capitalism.[9] And, as work that above all seeks to fashion a global heroic past for the Sierra Leonean nation-state, it highlights the transnational underpinnings of postcolonial nationalism.

Amistad Kata-Kata holds its own as a literary text, but the play's cultural importance stems significantly from its status as a work of public history. Readers and audiences should pay special attention to the figure of the grandmother who appears in the frame narrative and reappears periodically to comment on the action. In *Amistad Kata-Kata*'s opening framing scene, for instance, she laments the poor state of historical memory in Sierra Leone, going so far as to declare that public amnesia about resistance figures like Sengbe Pieh stands as a root cause of many of the country's social and economic ills. Without overtly suggesting that contemporary Sierra Leoneans should follow Sengbe Pieh's example of armed uprising, she nevertheless asserts that proper memorialization of those who resisted tyranny will go a long way toward improving the quality of life in the present. The pronouncement serves both to introduce the *Amistad* history to Sierra Leonean audiences and to assert Haffner's perspective on the relationship between historical memory and collective well-being. In the same opening scene, the grandmother castigates her university-educated grandson for putting too much faith in written histories, which, according to her, are untested by the rigors of oral tradition and public debate. Like the narrative tradition lauded by the grandmother, *Amistad Kata-Kata* offered itself to audiences as oral history. And like the oral tradition, the Freetong Players tailored individual performances to their audiences. As a result, few performances were identical, but each amplified the same themes. In several important ways, *Amistad Kata-Kata* set a template for the plays to follow.

The Amistad Revolt

Yulisa Amadu Maddy (1936–2014) premiered his play, *The Amistad Revolt*, at the University of Iowa in April 1993. He would stage it one more time, two years later, with the title *Give Us Free—The Amistad Revolt*, at Morris Brown College. Based on the success of these stagings and on Maddy's reputation as a playwright and novelist, Steven Spielberg flew Maddy to Los Angeles for discussions about developing the play into a screenplay for what would become his film. For undisclosed reasons, Maddy walked away from the negotiations, replaced by the American screenwriter David Franzoni, whose screenplay focuses the greater part of its narrative conflict on the redemption of its White American protagonists.

The Amistad Revolt stands as one of the final complete works in Maddy's career of writing and directing for the stage. His first four plays were published by Heinemann's African Writers Series in 1971 under the title *Obasai and Other Plays*. Two years later Heinemann brought out his novel *No Past, No Present, No Future*. Throughout the 1970s and 1980s, Maddy continued to write and stage plays, performed primarily by his drama company Gbakanda Afrikan Tiata. All of Maddy's productions, including *The Amistad Revolt*, share a commitment to exposing injustice and advancing the national struggle for freedom and dignity. In addition to working in stage drama, Maddy trained and directed the Zambian National Dance Troupe for Expo '70, in Japan, and the Sierra Leonean National Dance Troupe for FESTAC '77, in Nigeria. During the nearly three-decade period he spent in exile following his imprisonment related to the staging of *Big Berrin*, Maddy also taught drama in Nigeria and the United States. In 2007, he returned to Sierra Leone, where he remained until his death in 2014.

Like Haffner's before him and de'Souza George's after, Maddy's play narrates the events of the *Amistad* rebellion and its legal aftermath from the perspective of its Mende protagonists, depicting their uprising as a story of heroic struggle in which the enslaved maintain the unambiguous right to use violence in order to secure their liberty. And like the other two plays, the bulk of its action takes place on board the *Amistad*, in the Connecticut prison, and in the U.S. Supreme Court

Introduction: Staging the *Amistad*

chambers. With the exception of two fictionalized African American characters, the play puts the key historical figures on stage. In his obituary for the playwright, literary critic and fellow Sierra Leonean Eustace Palmer writes that Maddy enjoyed a "profound knowledge of what the theater was capable of, what worked and what did not, and the innovations that could be made."[10] This understanding is evident in *The Amistad Revolt*'s complex narrative arc, its frequent time shifts—often signaled by lighting and spatial organization—and ambitious thematics, all highly demanding on the sixty or more performers who appear on stage. But while Maddy takes advantage of the disproportionately greater technological and stage resources available to him in the United States (recorded sounds, visual projections, spotlighting, and so on) than would have been available to Haffner or de'Souza George in Freetown, the script never comes across as so reliant on them that the play could not have been staged in Sierra Leone.

For all the thematic and narrative similarities to *Amistad Kata-Kata*, *The Amistad Revolt* is distinguished from the earlier stage production by its more extensive incorporation of the written record. Like Haffner and de'Souza George, Maddy quotes directly from Andrew Judson's and John Quincy Adams's courtroom transcripts and Kale's letter to Adams, in which the child captive expresses so heartbreakingly his agony in face of America's racial hypocrisies. But Maddy takes his intertextuality a significant step further. In addition to drafting dialogue from nineteenth-century legal records and personal correspondence, Maddy borrows fictionalized characters, narrative conflicts, and entire conversations and interior monologues from Barbara Chase-Riboud's 1989 historical novel about the *Amistad* rebellion, *Echo of Lions*. The most significant of Maddy's adaptations from the novel include the incorporation of its fictionalized characters Henry Braithwaite and his daughter Vivian Braithwaite; its attention to District Court Judge Andrew Judson's prior involvement in the Prudence Crandall case; and its shared characterization of John Quincy Adams as being haunted by having been president of a slave-holding republic. Additionally, Maddy's play replicates some of the novel's narrative architecture and its linking of racial and gender inequality. So extensive are Maddy's borrowings from *Echo of Lions* that his surviving family and Barbara Chase-Riboud agreed that it would be most appropriate to publish the play as an adaptation of her novel.

By no means does the play's status as a partial adaptation of another literary text make it less compelling critically or aesthetically. Quite the opposite, in fact. Much of the *The Amistad Revolt*'s richness stems directly from the way that it incorporates primary source documents and fictional representations as equivalent records. At the most basic level, Maddy's inclusion of fictional material as a historical source in its own right highlights the erasure of the slave rebel's voice in Black Atlantic history. Apart from Kale's letter and the brief courtroom testimony of the few Amistads chosen to speak, rarely in the court records, missionary archives, newspaper accounts, diaries, and other archival documents can Sengbe Pieh's voice or that of any of the other rebels be found. This absence is just as true for the Amistads as for Gabriel Prosser, Denmark Vesey, Nat Turner, and the thousands of other protagonists in slave rebellions, large and small, in Africa, on board slave ships, or in the Americas. By turning to a fictional source for representations of those voices, Maddy only further highlights their profound absence in the public historical record. Like so many other authors of neo-slave narratives, Maddy also fills this vacuum, of course, with his own fictionalization of the expansive private lives of the *Amistad* slave rebels, imagining likely conversations, feelings of trauma, and sources of resilience, but always in transatlantic dialogue with Chase-Riboud's "historical" source text. A second effect of giving a novel equal footing as a nineteenth-century document is to call attention to the textuality of the nineteenth-century archival materials. Those historical documents were produced by lawyers, judges, journalists, abolitionists, missionaries, and diarists who, no matter their views on slavery, were never free from the ideologies of race and civilization of their era. By giving equal credence to a twentieth-century novel by an African American writer, Maddy suggests that the available primary sources are no less fictional than a contemporary novel and that a contemporary novel can be no less factual than court records, newspaper reports, and the like. Haffner does something similar when he has the grandmother in

Introduction: Staging the *Amistad*

Amistad Kata-Kata's frame narrative question the reliability of written records. But Maddy is perhaps the more radical in turning to fiction to critique the racism of the archive and to locate voices lost to history.

The other significant difference between *The Amistad Revolt* and the two other plays in this volume is its deeper engagement with the psychosubjective effects of antebellum American racism on its West African protagonists. From the opening scene to the last, the mutineers' struggle to comprehend and resist their racialization is made a central thematic focus. This is not to say that Haffner and de'Souza George ignore the effects of racism and racialization on the mutineers but rather that Maddy highlights to a much greater extent the traumas they induce. At a moment of what is perhaps his most acute despondency, Maddy's Sengbe accuses even his supporters of viewing him as "an unwelcome nigger, to be disposed of in any way as soon as possible." The greater focus on racism and subjectivity stems in part from the influence of Chase-Riboud's novel. Maddy borrows the Braithwaites, her fictional African American father and daughter, using them in much the same way Chase-Riboud does to root the Amistads' legal battle, which grew increasingly focused on esoteric questions of international trade law and executive power, in the cultures of American race relations. In the play as in the novel, the Braithwaites help Sengbe Pieh and the other Amistads understand the racial dynamics of their ordeal, naming the Amistads' humiliations as racism and historicizing that racism as one of the foundational contradictions of American society. In return, the Amistads offer the African Americans a glimpse of a life and subjectivity untainted by the daily degradations that define Black experience in the United States. Each ultimately helps the other resist the pressures to internalize Western racial ideologies. The extensive focus on race is also very much of a piece with Maddy's oeuvre. From his earliest plays, to his novel *No Past, No Present, No Future* (1973), and to his coauthored scholarly study of children's literature, colonial racism and its internalization by Africans on the African continent and in the diaspora was central to his writing. *The Amistad Revolt* is especially fascinating in this respect not only because it offers one of Maddy's most nuanced psychological portraits of the racialization of Africans displaced to

England or America, but also because it represents a rare direct transatlantic dialogue between Sierra Leonean and African American writers on race, the meanings of enslavement, and resistance.

The Broken Handcuff

The final play in this collection is Reverend Raymond E. D. de'Souza George's *The Broken Handcuff*. Like Haffner, de'Souza George credits Joseph Opala, his colleague at Fourah Bay College, for sparking his fascination with the 1839 revolt, and in the play's treatment of heroic struggle and Sierra Leone's geopolitical impact, it echoes Opala's lectures and Haffner's earlier rendition. And like *Amistad Kata-Kata*, it debuted at the British Council auditorium in Freetown. De'Souza George staged it one more time, with a reduced cast, at the 1994 Victoria Canadian fringe theater festival. It has not been performed since. *The Broken Handcuff* ultimately shies away from *Amistad Kata-Kata*'s celebratory air, cloaking the rebellion narrative instead with a bleaker, more dystopic vision. The play comes to its climatic close in the U.S. Supreme Court chambers with the announcement of the Amistads' legal victory, but any triumph is undercut in the same scene by a slip-of-the-tongue reference to Chief Justice Roger Brooke Taney, whose Supreme Court issued the *Dred Scott* decision just a few years later, and by a reminder of Sengbe Pieh's discovery upon his return to Mendeland of the likely enslavement of his entire family. De'Souza George also devotes significantly more stage time to the Mende-speaking Africans who collaborated with the coastal slave dealers, depicting them not so much as one-dimensional craven monsters than as individuals motivated by the all-too-recognizably human qualities of jealousy, grievance, and ego. And, moreover, instead of emphasizing the civic well-being to be gained by celebrating forgotten resistance heroes, *The Broken Handcuff* dwells more on "how much of our history and culture were swept away" because of the inability or unwillingness to acknowledge the legacies of enslavement.

A significant measure of the difference from Haffner's play must be attributed to the changed historical context. In 1991, three years after *Amistad Kata-Kata*'s debut, Sierra Leone suffered the first wave of armed raids

Introduction: Staging the *Amistad*

by a rebel militia calling itself the Revolutionary United Front/Sierra Leone (RUF/SL). After remaining relatively contained in the south and east of the country for a year and a half, the RUF/SL launched a major offensive in September 1992 that culminated in the capture of a large diamond-mining concession. From that point on, the already weakly equipped government forces found it increasingly difficult to check the rebel militia's spread. In contrast to Haffner, writing only six years earlier, de'Souza George offers a narrative about the *Amistad* rebellion that functions much less to will into being a more civic-minded future than to question how Sierra Leone could have fallen so far from its modest prosperity at the point of political independence and let its ambitious postcolonial dreams slip away in such violent fashion.

Born in 1947, Raymond de'Souza George has played a leading role as a writer, director, actor, and mentor for young theater professionals coming up through the Institute of African Studies at Fourah Bay College, where he spent his professional career. As a founding member of the influential drama company Tabule Theater, de'Souza George acted in a leading role in Dele Charley's *Blood of a Stranger*, the best original drama award winner at FESTAC '77, the festival of black arts held in Lagos, Nigeria, which saw the staging of now-canonical plays like Ngũgĩ wa Thiong'o and Ngũgĩ wa Mirii's critique of neocolonialism *I Will Marry When I Want*. De'Souza George's own scripts include the Krio-language play *Bobo Lef*, which was performed at the London International Theater Festival in 1983, and the English-language work *On Trial for a Will*, plays that take aim at the corruption of Sierra Leone's political leaders and the failure of the country's citizens to stop it. Like other Sierra Leonean playwrights of his generation, de'Souza George has refused to assign external figures such as Euro-American slave traders and British colonizers sole blame for the country's ills, preferring instead to lay a portion of the responsibility in the hands of the country's own precolonial and postindependence elite. De'Souza George does not, however, propose that Africa has met the West on equal footing. Suggesting that Euro-American slave traders would not have been able to purchase slaves if there were not Africans willing to sell their fellow Africans, de'Souza George asks, "If the West came to

Sierra Leone and wanted to buy [slaves] and the Sierra Leoneans didn't sell, who would they have bought?" At the same time, he nevertheless insists that slavery is only possible when transatlantic economic conditions are defined by a stark "difference in levels of opportunity."[11] One of the tensions giving his writing its richness stems from the challenge of representing that local culpability without losing sight of the relative socioeconomic disadvantage structuring it.

In a significant departure from Haffner's earlier staging of the *Amistad* history, de'Souza George develops *The Broken Handcuff*'s thematics through its sophisticated aesthetic architecture as much as through plot and character. Readers and theater companies interested in staging the play thus need to pay close attention to its use of allegory and metaphor, its interplay of languages (English, Krio, and Mende), and its Brechtian theatricality. Before we are ever even introduced to the *Amistad* revolt protagonists, for example, part 1, scene 3 stages an allegorical encounter set in the ancestral world of the nation-state to suggest that Sierra Leone's common historical narrative of itself has blinded its citizens to the root sources of the avariciousness and exploitation plaguing the country. As the scene begins, the lights come up to reveal a confrontation between the first colonial governor and six anticolonial nationalists from Sierra Leone's colonial and early independence past. In their cataloguing of the physical and epistemological violence done by colonialism, the anticolonial nationalists end up unable to escape the binary relation of colonizer-colonized or to produce a useful critique of the root causes of the contemporary exploitation depicted in the play's opening frame. At the point when the anticolonialists' tactics appear to have reached their discursive limits, Sengbe Pieh, standing all the while in richly metaphoric shadow at the edge of the stage, steps into the light to authoritatively assert that the country's myopic focus on its colonial history has blinded it to other equally significant genealogies, including, most obviously, the transatlantic slave trade. Similarly, in a second example, de'Souza George implicitly challenges Ngũgĩ wa Thiong'o's contention that African languages give the most authentic and uncorrupted expression to African cultures. By giving the only African-language lines in the play to the characters who have most fully embraced the Atlantic trade's devaluation of

Introduction: Staging the *Amistad*

human life—the Mende slave-catchers—the play seems to suggest that so deeply corrupted was Mende society and culture that the Mende language itself speaks the language of enslavement and alienation. Despite his play's bleak tone and outlook, de'Souza George never loses sight of the fact that the *Amistad* revolt tells the story of resistance to the seemingly overwhelming forces of exploitation in a globalized world. For as much as the *Amistad* rebels' experience in his telling points to Sierra Leone's amnesia about its exploited and self-exploitative past, the play asserts that freedom and dignity are worth fighting for and, indeed, must continuously be fought for. For all the differences that distinguish *Amistad Kata-Kata*, *The* Amistad *Revolt*, and *The Broken Handcuff*, they share this assertion. And they share the assertion that Sierra Leone, with all of its political and economic crises and with its dream of decolonization painfully deferred, is an idea absolutely worth defending. Their plays, too, serve as a reminder that Sierra Leone remained, and remains still, a work in progress, knee deep in the necessary labor of fashioning a past to define its present and energize its future. While stage drama has lost some of the dominance it enjoyed in the second half of the twentieth century, the *Amistad* plays' distinct cultural labors continue to exert outsized influence over Sierra Leone's literary production, especially in prose fiction, which has blossomed in the postwar first decades of the twenty-first century. In novels no less committed to opening up Sierra Leone's future, Aminata Forna, Eustace Palmer, Onipede Hollist, and J. Sorie Conteh have taken up and extended the three playwrights' attention to the country's pasts for both the root causes of its current conflicts and the cultural, social, and historical resources required to achieve the nation's promise. Sitting at the forefront of this literary zeitgeist, the three *Amistad* plays offer a powerful reminder about how literature remains a vital force in the ongoing struggle for independence and equality.

Notes on the Texts

Charlie Haffner and Raymond de'Souza George provided typescript copies of *Amistad Kata-Kata* and *The Broken Handcuff* and consulted closely for their publication in this volume. Yulisa Amadu Maddy passed away shortly before I began to assemble the plays. His personal records and manuscripts remain currently in significant disarray in Sierra Leone and England. For these reasons, the version of *The Amistad Revolt* that I have included here is based on a script provided by Ansa Akyea, the Ghanaian actor who played Sengbe Pieh in the University of Iowa performances in 1993. Akyea's manuscript is extensively marked up, with passages of dialogue and song, some quite long, crossed out or added by hand. I worked with Akyea to produce a script that conforms as closely as his memory allows to the version of the play that Yulisa Amadu Maddy directed. Posthumous publication is always fraught, but I am confident that Maddy would have approved this text. I would like to note, however, that even the published script of *Amistad Kata-Kata* challenges accepted standards for what constitutes an authoritative text. During the height of *Amistad Kata-Kata*'s popularity, Haffner and his theater troupe, the Freetong Players, rarely treated the script as a fixed text. They routinely revised dialogue and adapted individual stage performances to take advantage of differential resources or to address different types of audiences. *Amistad Kata-Kata* was, and remains to them, a dynamic work in progress.

In my preparation of the plays for publication, I remained minimally interventionist in my editing. I corrected obvious typographical errors and made minor changes to formatting to ensure that the plays conform to general play publishing standards. Readers and actors should assume that all punctuation, language usage, and style, no matter how nonstandard, are intentional. Sierra Leonean English typically employs British spellings (e.g., honour, centre, etc.), as is reflected in Raymond de'Souza George's script. Charlie Haffner's play appears here with American spellings in conformity with the typescript he gave me. Maddy's original manuscript mixed British and American spellings, with the same word occasionally spelled both ways and with no obvious organizing logic. Given that the majority of Maddy's spellings were American and given that he wrote and only ever staged the play in the United States, his family and I chose to use American spellings throughout.

Introduction: Staging the *Amistad*

Readers of Maddy's play should also note his differential capitalization of racial terms. In every instance, he decapitalizes the word "white" when referring to European Americans, and, with few exceptions, capitalizes "Black" and "Negro." The differential capitalization would remain indistinguishable aurally, of course, but, visually, it ascribes with unusual force the humanity and dignity to people of African descent that the proper noun denotes and forces White readers to confront their own assumptions and privileges. Where the manuscript did not capitalize these terms, I considered the context and made a judgment about whether the decapitalization was intentional or a likely typographical error and revised accordingly. For instance, when Judge Judson spews his racist venom about race pride I chose to leave his use of the word "blacks" uncapitalized, as it appears in the manuscript, because it signifies Judson's view of Africans and African Americans as unworthy of proper noun status. But Maddy also leaves "white" uncapitalized in the same lines of dialogue, which comes across visually as Maddy's attempt to subvert the violence of Judson's racist rhetoric, a rhetoric that certainly had not disappeared from American life by the 1990s.

Timeline

16th century	Transatlantic slave trade begins along the Upper Guinea Coast.
1787	"Province of Freedom," near today's Freetown, first settled by "Black Poor" liberated slaves living in England.
1792	Freetown established by second wave of liberated slaves from the Americas.
1808	Sierra Leone declared a British Crown Colony.
1808–17	Major Atlantic powers sign treaties to abolish transatlantic slave trade.
1808–60	British naval patrols enforcing treaties settle Africans liberated from illegal slaving vessels in Freetown regardless of their origin.
Apr. 1839	Slave ship *Teçora* sets sail from Lomboko carrying Sengbe Pieh and other *Amistad* rebels to Cuba. Slave factories around Lomboko were sending about 2,000 Africans per year to the Americas at this time.
June 28, 1839	Carrying Sengbe Pieh and other *Amistad* rebels, *La Amistad* departs Havana for Puerto Principe.
July 1, 1839	*Amistad* rebellion, followed by two months at sea.
Aug. 26, 1839	Lt. Gedney and crew of USS *Washington* take command of the *Amistad*.
Sept. 1839–Sept. 1849	*Amistad*-focused District and Circuit Court trials.

TIMELINE

Mar. 9, 1841	Supreme Court rules in favor of the *Amistad* rebels.
Nov. 1841–Jan. 1842	*The Gentleman* returns the surviving Amistads and members of the American Missionary Society to Sierra Leone.
1898	Bai Bureh leads war in opposition to British efforts to assert colonial control of areas outside Freetown.
1920s–1950s	Period marked by increasing anticolonial nationalist demands for political independence.
Apr. 27, 1961	Sierra Leone gains political independence from British colonial rule. Milton Margai named first prime minister.
1978	Siaka Stevens declares one-party rule. Period marked by global economic crises, political misrule, and increasing culture of corruption, which lead to a long period of economic decline.
1985	Stevens's handpicked successor Joseph Saidu Momoh elected president; Momoh welcomes International Monetary Fund reforms; economy continues to erode.
1988	Charlie Haffner debuts *Amistad Kata-Kata* in Freetown at the British Council auditorium.
Mar. 23, 1991	The Revolutionary United Front/Sierra Leone (RUF/SL) launches first armed attacks in southern Sierra Leone, initiating a decade-long war.
Apr. 29, 1992	Military coup topples Momoh's government; widespread optimism that military government will bring a quick end to the war.
1993	Grassroots art movement makes *Amistad* revolt leader Sengbe Pieh a central icon in public murals designed to foster national pride in opposition to RUF/SL.
1993	Yulisa Amadu Maddy debuts *The Amistad Revolt* at the University of Iowa.
1994	Raymond de'Souza George debuts *The Broken Handcuff* in Freetown at the British Council auditorium.
Jan. 18, 2002	The war is declared over and disarmament complete.

Sengbe Pieh

A Ballad

BY CHARLIE HAFFNER

Sengbe Pieh

Yu yeri bot slavery,
Yu yeri bot Sengbe Pieh,
Yu yeri bot Amistad, Amistad Kata-Kata,
Sengbe Pieh nar Sa Lone man,
E born nar Pujehun,
E mama nar Mende, e papa nar Mende,
Way e twenty-six years, 1839,
Nar Im dem kaych am, den sell am to slavery,
King Mana Shaka nar im been sell am,
De Vai king of Pujehun,
Siaka Stevens im granpapa,
Dem pull dem nar Sierra Leone,
In en im compin dem,
Den ship dem go Cuba, Havana de capital,
Nay day dem buy dem,
For ker dem go Principe,
49 Sierra Leoneans, 3 titi en 1 borbor,
Dem ire wan ship, nar in name Amistad,
For ship dem from Havana to Puerto Principe,
Amistad O, Amistad O
Nar so de ship name,
A.M.I.S.T.A.D.—Amistad.

Sengbe Pieh lead in kompin dem,
49 Sierra Leoneans, 3 titi en 1 borbor,
Den attack de Amistad, den ib Kata-Kata,
Den kill de captain, den kill de cook,
Den tie-tie den owner,
Den mass-mass den troat,

Sengbe order de owner dem,
For sail back to Africa,
Back to Sierra Leone,
De land of the rising sun,
Back to Sierra Leone,
Back to Sierra Leone,
Den order de Amistad,
Back to Sierra Leone.

As fate would have it,
Man proposes, God disposes,
Den slam nar United States,
Nar dey dem kaych dem, de Amerikan Navy,
Dem put dem nar kot, insaye United States,
Dem charge dem with murder,
Dem charge dem with piracy,
Dem call dem cannibals, dem call dem savages,
As fate would have it,
Man proposes, God disposes,
De Amistad win dem case,
Out of den 49, 3 titi and 1 borbor,
11 been done rest in peace,
Papa God been done take den lif,
So Sengbe Pieh e en e kompin dem,
38 Sierra Leoneans, 3 titi and 1 borbor,
Wit 5 missionaries, Amerikin missionaries,
Slam insaye Govment Waf, 1842.

Back to Sierra Leone,
Back to Sierra Leone,
Back to Sierra Leone,
De land of the rising sun.

Wetin Ah want for tell una,
Fellow Sierra Leoneans, brothers and sisters,

Sengbe Pieh: A Ballad

Our leaders of tomorrow,
Nar Sengbe Pieh dem bring dis mission,
Way start wok nar Shengbe 1843,
Dem for name nar Mende mission,
Dem change to U.B.C. den change to E.U.B.,
Now nar de U.M.C.
Den opin Albert Academy,
Den opin Harford School,
Den shayb-shayb scholarships,
Den don gi we biships,
Den gi we Prime Minister,
Den give we president from Albert Academy,
Yu yeri bot slavery,
Yu yeri bot Sengbe Pieh,
Yu yeri bot Amistad, Amistad Kata-Kata.

Amistad Kata-Kata

BY CHARLIE HAFFNER

Cast
(In order of appearance)

Student	Sessi
Grandma	Kale
Herald	Captain Ferrer
Adherents	Celestino
Priest	Two Sailors
Shrine Attendants	Jasabe
Two Boys	Bona
Chief Priest	Kai
Ghost	1st Captain
Sengbe Pieh	Comptroller
Voices, Villagers	2nd Captain
Girls	Lieutenant Gedney
Kagne	Lieutenant Meade
Reira	John Quincy Adams
Slave Auction Guards	Adams's Chef
Ruiz	Lewis Tappan
Montez	Reverend Simeon Jocelyn
Antonio	Joshua Leavitt
Montez's Assistant	Attorney General
Sa	Baldwin
Kimbo	Judge
Gabro	Townspeople, Chorus
Fulleh	

SCENE ONE

A bush path near the village of Komende, Sierra Leone, West Africa (mid-1980s). Grandma, a woman in her eighties, and a young college Student enter, deep in conversation. Grandma's laughter soon replaces the memorial dirge that fills the air.

GRANDMA: *(Coughing.)* Soon we shall be in Komende—the home of Sengbe Pieh. It was along this same path that Sengbe was captured over 2,000 moons ago. We are quite early, in time for the ceremony . . .

STUDENT: Yes, Grandma, the ceremony is tonight. I am happy I made it after all . . .

GRANDMA: Are you? *(Laughter again.)* Please help me with some tobacco. (Student *helps to fill and ignite the pipe. Grandma takes a few satisfying puffs. Clears her throat.*) You see, my son, our people have a tradition which is based on the belief that a person survives after death, and it is this surviving personality spirit that enters the land of the dead.

STUDENT: I agree with you, Grandma. From my readings, I have discovered that nearly all African tribes have some kind of ancestral culture. I think the Mendes of Africa call it Tenjamei or so . . .

GRANDMA: You are quite right, my son. In order for the spirit of the dead ancestor to "enter his new country," that spirit has to first cross a river. It is here that the Tenjamei or "crossing the river" rites come in.

STUDENT: Ehhnn . . . Grandma, let me take this point down. *(He takes out a notebook from his raffia bag and writes in it.)* . . . Eh . . . Grandma, go on, please . . .

GRANDMA: *(Ridicules.)* Ah . . . you people are always writing . . . our bookmen of today! *(Laughter.)*

STUDENT: Grandma, please don't laugh . . . you have just made a very relevant point. Please go on.

GRANDMA: Alright . . . alright . . . the spirit cannot cross the river unless these rites have been carried out. So it is important that surviving relatives are willing to perform them.

STUDENT: *(Still writing,)* Hhnn . . . otherwise, Grandma?

GRANDMA: Otherwise, to deny a dead person these rites is tantamount to condemning the spirit and thus be haunted by it . . .

STUDENT: . . . Is that true, Grandma?

GRANDMA: You ask me if that is true? Can your Grandma tell a lie? Even if it is a lie, write it down . . . go on, write this one down. Our ancestors can be angry with us and, as a result, become vengeful towards us because they were wronged during their lifetime or after . . .

STUDENT: So misfortune suffered today by say . . . a person, or a family . . .

GRANDMA: . . . or even a nation can be a sign of ancestral displeasure and a warning to the parties concerned that they must look closely into their conduct—toward their ancestral spirits.

STUDENT: *(Still writing.)* Hhnn . . . I see . . .

GRANDMA: *(Ridicules.)* What do you see? You see nothing, son. You bookmen and leaders of today fail to see that it is our ancestors that offer us guidance and counseling throughout our never ending stream of life. But when a child is well fed, does he not look upon the grave as an ordinary heap of earth?

STUDENT: What is that, Grandma?

GRANDMA: You just go on copying. As far as I am concerned, Sengbe Pieh is about the most influential Sierra Leonean that ever lived. It is a great tragedy that he is not remembered by his own people who have still not realized the importance of using him as a symbol of national pride.

STUDENT: Surely, Grandma, ever since I was far younger than this, I have heard names, Africans of other countries like Shaka the Zulu, Sundiata Keita, Mansa Musa, Osie Tutu, yes . . . . . !!! The Samoris and the Lion of Judah, who pitched their strength against the white man—boldly trying to keep them away from Africa.

GRANDMA: Well, my son, we too have our Bai Burehs, our Manga Sewas, our Ndawas, Kai Londos, Alimany Sulukus, Madam Yokos, and not to mention Sengbe Pieh. But the truth will be out tonight. A snail may run, but cannot avoid its shell. The truth never falters. As from tonight, the world will know who Sengbe Pieh was. Come, let's go . . .

Grandma *exits*. Student *stays on*.

STUDENT: (*Flipping through his pages excitedly.*) . . . Ehh . . . Grandma, please wait, let me check what I have down so far. (*He addresses the audience.*) Ladies and Gentlemen, I am a student of the school of theatre arts. I am doing a research on a lost Sierra Leonean. I want to write a play about his life and times, and a song that will tell of his heroic deeds so that the world . . . (Grandma *returns.*)

GRANDMA: My son, come now, let's go . . .

STUDENT: Ehh. Grandma, please let me check what I have down so far . . .

GRANDMA: Oh son, come on . . .

STUDENT: Grandma, just a quick run-down . . . ehh . . . (*Flipping through his pages excitedly.*) . . . Ehh . . . Sengbe Pieh—born in Sierra Leone, West Africa . . . 1813 . . . a Mende man from the south region of his country, a farmer . . . son of a town chief—a wife and two children . . . eh . . . it was in January 1839 . . .

GRANDMA: Son, let's go, food is ready . . .

STUDENT: Hhnn? Did you say food is ready, Grandma?

GRANDMA: (*Grabbing* Student *by his arm and pulling him.*) Yes, food is ready. Let's go or it will get cold. See, the sun is going down. There is not much time left.

As they exit, a dirge takes over, increasingly into a crescendo and fades away on blackout.

SCENE TWO

A typical African grave site in the dead of midnight. In the background are sounds of howling, moans, dry cries, and barking blending with fetish rhythms. The Herald *emerges slowly from behind the grave. He carries a staff in his right hand and a bell in the left. He starts a slow dance which develops as the rhythm intensifies. Abruptly, lifting his hand in the air, he brings the music to a stop.*

HERALD: (*In a clear, stern voice.*) Oh . . . Ngaywoh . . . let it reach you. Let it reach to Kaanga. Let it reach to Ginagaa and to Ndorgdohuswi, Nbondaysia, Kiniayasia and the great sons of men on earth. Here we are again, today. We are here at your graveside, for sickness is threatening us. We cry in vain for help. We ail and suffer. Poverty comes as rain and calamity engulfs us in flames. Agbohloh wants to go Bondo,[1] but there is no waist to tie the jigida. Trohki wants to box, but his hand is too short. Hearts are unclean—Ngaywoh, hearts are unclean. Evil plotters multiply like mosquitoes in open swampland. The dog flirts with the lioness, not knowing that his death has come. Layvay informs us that we have wronged our great ancestors and we have, ourselves, condemned their spirits to remain on earth and be haunted by them. We have come to beg to pull the curse inflicted upon us, so that we can, hereafter, live in unity, peace, prosperity and freedom once more . . . . .

Exit. The fetish drums take over again. A group of Fetish Adherents *dance onto the stage, possessed. As the drums flare, the* Herald *dances in swiftly and, at his signal, the music stops, abruptly. He pitches a tune which the others take up and leads a fetish dance, which drives them into frenzy. He exits. Seconds later, the jingling of the hand bell marks the entry of the* Chief Priest, *in fetish dress, hat, and talisman. In front of the conjuring* Chief Priest, *stagger two* Shrine Attendants *side by side, possessed, carrying a bowl of red rice and a bulie (jug) of palm wine. The* Herald *guides the struggling adherents to their position.*

HERALD: (*To the possessed boys.*) Easy . . . Easy . . . great custodian of Ngaywoh, he steps forward . . . he who never tires . . . the most supreme . . . the most bounteous . . . he comes . . . he who accompanies the most divine . . . the most magnanimous . . . easy . . . he, the carrier of the bundle of the great guiding spirits must be stronger than strong . . . easy . . .

CHIEF PRIEST: (*Emphatically.*) Oh . . . you ancestors, the spirits of our fathers, and grandfathers, and great grandfathers, and great, great grandfathers, who make the end of the sea your abode . . . you ancestral spirits in the belly of the Earth—I call you forth. You the guardian spirit that watch over mortals, you fathers who can sleep no more—I summon you all—you Sengbe, Bureh, Yoko, Manga, Londo, Ndawa, Wallaci, Miltini, Siaka.[2] I invoke and convoke you and your attendant deities!!!

HERALD: Hiii . . . Hiii . . . he comes . . . he comes . . . the spirits have assembled . . . the great ancestors have descended . . . (*To the invisible spirits.*) Welcome, you assembled fathers from beyond the seas . . . we welcome you . . . (*Suddenly, he runs out.*)

CHIEF PRIEST: (*Pouring libation, offering red rice, and throwing kola nuts as a means of communication.*) Here, great fathers from beyond—we have called you here. Things are very difficult for us. We do not know. So, we ask. Speak to us . . . speak . . . speak . . . speak . . .

HERALD: (*Runs from behind the grave, dressed like a ghost. He jingles a hand bell and spins on the ground.*) Hiii . . . bbrr . . . bbrr . . . hiii . . . news . . . news . . . he comes . . . hot news . . . news from the dead . . . news from the ancestors, long forgotten . . . (*Fixes to a spot, listens, no clue, shakes his head, fixes to another spot, listens again, no sign, then suddenly.*) He comes . . . he is here . . . he comes . . .

Then, a Ghost, weeping and wailing, gives indication of his arrival.

CHIEF PRIEST: (*Fixing himself on the spot, half possessed, looking up at the ghost.*) Ahh . . . welcome . . . you are welcome . . . Sengbe Pieh . . . welcome . . . it's a long time we have not heard from you. Sengbe, welcome. You must be thirsty. Here is some water. Drink.

GHOST: (*Emphatically.*) No!!

CHIEF PRIEST: Sengbe, are you not thirsty? Drink.

GHOST: Ahn . . . ahn . . . I cannot drink.

CHIEF PRIEST: Pardon your children, Sengbe. Forgive us. You are our guiding spirit of the unknown—prompt to punish us whenever we transgress.

I am Gbanagbome, son of Kai Koni Sokogbana of Kpa Mende.
Please do not refuse our call. Here, Sengbe, take our good morning.

GHOST: Good morning. How are you and our people?

CHIEF PRIEST: So and so, Sengbe. How do you and your associates fare, over there.

GHOST: We are alive and well. They send you their regards.

CHIEF PRIEST: Sengbe, the living gathered here want to hear from you. You were a member of this community when you were captured and sold to slavery. Do you remember?

GHOST: Of course, I remember everything. I remember very well.

CHIEF PRIEST: Tell us, Sengbe, what happened. Stories have come and stories have gone, yet we do not know who to trust. Our children want to know and we cannot tell them. Help us, Sengbe. Let us right our wrongs, once and for all. Our cocoyam is white. We can no longer cover it. If I had known, always comes last. The cockroach does not go to market but it eats palm oil. Before it burns, let it soak more and more . . .

GHOST: Okay. Thank you. Thank you very much. You remind me of the Poro, once more. I will tell you. I will tell you, but let me hear the drums once again!! (*At one call by the* Herald, *all drums flare to a crescendo. The* Ghost *joins in the dance of frenzy. Then the music stops abruptly and the* Ghost *can he heard gasping as he begins to speak.*) Listen to my story. (*Pause.*) It was in my village of Romendi, in the middle of the dry season, 26 harmattans after I was born. I later came to learn from the white man that it was January, 1839. I was on my way to farm, early one morning, when I was ambushed by men, sent to capture me. But wait, let's see, I have an idea.

CHIEF PRIEST: What's the matter again, Sengbe?

GHOST: I have an idea. We can act out my story. Yes. Let us act out my story as if it were a play. We can help the student to start writing his play. For example, I need four men to lay an ambush for me and then eventually capture me after a hard fight—tie me up and drag me away. Who would want to be the men to capture me?

Amistad Kata-Kata

VOICE 1: Me...

GHOST: Yes.

VOICE 2: Me.

VOICE 3: I will try.

GHOST: What about you?

VOICE 4: Okay, let me try.

GHOST: Good. So you four know what to do... now, imagine it is in my village, on the way to my farm, early morning. Okay? Here is the village. You lay your ambush. I fall into it. We fight. You capture and tie me up and drag me way. Okay?

OTHERS: Yes. Okay.

GHOST: Now, what was I wearing? My shokoto. Okay? My ronko hat.[3] Yes. I was also hanging a goatskin bag, carrying a hoe and a cutlass. Yes. Now, let's go. I will begin...

Flashback on scene of capture. Four men ambush Sengbe—a big fight. Sengbe tougher than expected. The attackers resort to the use of ropes, sticks, and machetes before Sengbe is overpowered. His right hand is tied to his neck and he is heavily guarded as he is led away.

SENGBE: You see. If we act out my story, it will be better than if I tell it alone. So, we are going to need the people for my story.

VOICE 2: What type of people?

SENGBE: Those like me, who were the slaves.

VOICE 1: How many?

SENGBE: Fifty-three.

VOICE 3: Fifty-three? We cannot have fifty-three slaves to act. We have to adjust.

SENGBE: Yes. We have to adjust. I know. Just eight or ten slaves will do. There are also three girls between nine and eleven years and a boy, Kale—twelve years old. Kale is important, so let's have Kale.

Voice 2: We can also have one girl instead of three.

Sengbe: Yes. Let's have Kagne. Kagne is the important one. Who will be Kagne? (Girls *put their hands up.*) Let it be you. (*Indicating one.*) You will be one of the female dancers. We are going to have male and female dancers. Also, we need Spanish actors. Ruiz—Pedro we need the Captain of the ship—the cook, Celestino—cabin boy, Antonio. We also need white Americans for the committee. There were also many lawyers.

Voice 3: Then we need many people. So, we still have to adjust.

Voice 2: But we have no white men here. Who will play the white parts? Nobody speaks like an American here, or like the Spanish.

Voice 1: Yes, the white roles—nobody to play them. And their costumes, what were they like? We don't have them.

Sengbe: Okay, you are right. Don't worry. Come with me. Let us go prepare. I have my dead American friends with whom I have been hanging out. I will ask them to come and play the white roles. Let us not waste any more time. Let's go and prepare.

They break into a dance. Blackout.

SCENE THREE

A typical slave baracoon. Havana, Cuba—late June, 1839. An oblong enclosure without a roof. Slaves continue to enter. Men, women, and children come stumbling in, bumping into one another, chained and bound. Some are in pain, some angry, some drugged, others dumbed. Slave Guards supervise with whips and threats. Other slave Guards bring food—boiled rice, cassava, plantains, and palm oil. Other Guards use raw palm oil to anoint slaves' cracked skins. Then, Sengbe Pieh comes stumbling in, chained to an older man. Sengbe appears inwardly cool. He takes time to study each and what goes on around. He refuses food and water, when served. Suddenly, laughter is heard off stage. Enter Senor Reira, *the baracoon owner and wealthy slave merchant, and* Jose Ruiz, *a young Cuban dandy who comes bartering for slaves. Ruiz is a seasoned businessman who knows his trade. Accompanying Ruiz is* Antonio, *a black Cuban ladino*[4]—*carrying his briefcase.*

Amistad Kata-Kata

REIRA: *(In heavy Cuban tongue.)* . . . Eh . . . Senor Jose Ruiz.

RUIZ: Call me Pepe. That is the name everybody calls me . . . eh . . . *(Introducing* Antonio.*)* This is Antonio. He is the cabin boy of . . .

REIRA: Captain Ramon Ferrer—owner and captain of *La Amistad*.

RUIZ: *(Shocked.)* Do you know Captain Ramon Ferrer?

REIRA: Which slave dealer on this island does not know Captain Ramon Ferrer, his cabin boy, Antonio, and his mulatto cook, Celestino? *(Giggles.)* . . . Eh . . . Pepe, do you say that you are seeking slaves to add to your family estate plantation?

RUIZ: *(Boastfully.)* Yes, indeed, Senor Reira. I am seeking slaves to add to our family estate plantation in Puerto Principe. About fifty.

REIRA: Ahh . . . good man. Sugar estate plantation?

Ruiz: Sugar estate plantation.

REIRA: Good. Good man. Go ahead, Pepe. Choose. Choose fifty. It's all yours. Go on. Choose fifty. Right?

RUIZ: Right.

They shake hands and Reira exits. With the help of assistants with practiced hands, Jose Ruiz *goes over the slaves—each of the men, skipping the women and children. He opens their mouths, checks their nostrils, examines for venereal diseases and anal problems. He thumps and thwacks them. He picks out forty-nine young men, including* Sengbe Pieh. *Satisfied, he calls out.*

RUIZ: Senor Reira! . . . forty-nine! . . . Senor Reira! . . . finito!

REIRA: *(Dashing in.)* Yaaa!

RUIZ: Forty-nine, Senor. I have chosen forty-nine.

REIRA: *(Disappointed.)* Only forty-nine? What's the matter, Pepe? At first you said fifty, so I told you to choose fifty. Now, you choose only forty-nine?

RUIZ: Yes, only forty-nine. How much for each slave?

REIRA: Six hundred fifty dollars each.

RUIZ: Six hundred fifty dollars each? Too much, Senor.

REIRA: Not too much, Senor. See, these slaves have just arrived from Africa, west coast. Direct from the warehouse, my friend Pepe . . .

RUIZ: I give you three hundred fifty dollars each.

REIRA: Too small, Pepe. Too small. Pay six hundred dollars.

RUIZ: Still too much. Take four hundred dollars.

REIRA: No. Four hundred dollars each—not good for me. I will take five hundred dollars each. You see, Pepe, if you intend to use them in your family estate plantation, as you say, they are worth the price. These are young men—strong black Africans, healthy, not ladinos born in Cuba. You know that young, healthy, black men, just arriving from Africa always cost more on the slave market . . .

RUIZ: Okay. Four hundred fifty dollars—last I can pay, Senor. The last.

REIRA: Right. Four hundred fifty dollars each. Pay.

RUIZ: So, for forty-nine, I give you . . . eh . . .

REIRA: *(Without thinking.)* Twenty-two thousand fifty dollars.

RUIZ: Correct. Good man. Good dealer.

Ruiz signals to Antonio, *who comes forward with briefcase, which he opens. He takes out money and counts before handing over to* Reira. *As Reira is cross-checking, another slave dealer,* Pedro Montez—*in his fifties—enters.*

MONTEZ: *(Directly.)* How much for that boy? *(Pointing to* Kale.*)* Oh . . . *(Noticing the girls.)* and those three girls?

REIRA: You want only children, Senor?

MONTEZ: Yes. How much for each?

REIRA: Four hundred fifty dollars each.

MONTEZ: Ah . . . come on, Senor. These are children. Not so much . . .

REIRA: Yes, children today—adult tomorrow, Senor Montez. With the chance of making many, many more children, who can also give you more and more.

Amistad Kata-Kata

MONTEZ: I know but four hundred fifty dollars, too much—and I want to buy all four children. (*Proceeds to examine the children just like* Ruiz *did.*)

REIRA: You see, Senor, these are all fresh, healthy, just arrived from Africa. They are worth the price. You will not regret your bargain, Senor Montez. Look, our friend Pepe just bought these forty-nine young men for his family plantation in Puerto Principe.

MONTEZ: Me too. I come from Puerto Principe. We want to experiment—to see what it is like to raise children on our family estate.

REIRA: Well, try these, Senor. You may not have this chance again. You may never see children like these, direct from Africa, again. Cuba is now filled with ladino and mulatto slaves born here and they are not as strong as the real Africans . . .

MONTEZ: Okay, you win. So, for these four children, I give you . . .

REIRA: One thousand eight hundred dollars.

MONTEZ: Okay. Here, Senor Reira, my good friend. (*Signals to his* Assistant *to open suitcase in front of* Reira *revealing contents.*) Take half a dozen bars of silver, sixty-foot length of cotton cloth, two guns, a packet of gun powder, four pounds of tobacco, and a box of Santa Maria rum.

REIRA: Take the boy. Take the three girls. (*Receives the suitcase. Both parties pleased.*) If you decide to take them to the slave market, they will be worth twice.

MONTEZ: I told you, it's for our family estate in Puerto Principe!

REIRA: Okay, Senor, okay. I believe you. No problema.

RUIZ: (*Instructing.*) Hey! Antonio! Get the cargo ready. We have to leave now. We will set sail this night for Puerto Principe.

REIRA: Eh . . . Pepe Pedro . . . listen ... (*Pulls him aside.*) Go to the government building in town, and ask for Capitan General. Get a passport from him to transport your cargo to Puerto Principe by sea. You will have to see the Capitan General specially, you know . . . for the deal . . . I mean the passports. You know the game . . . Okay? Once you receive the passport with Spanish names for them, you pretend that they are ladinos born in Cuba, okay? Understand?

Lights turn on Slaves *being fed by* Guards *after they are properly chained around their necks, waists, and hands in preparation for the long, night march toward the coast.*

ANTONIO: *(To other assistants.)* Let's go find something to eat. The journey is going to be long. The slaves are many and we may not be able to rest. *(Cross-checking the* Slaves *again, they exit, leaving the* Slaves *all by themselves—the oldest, tied to* Sengbe, *is the first to speak.)*

SA: Bi-lai-wa lai-tha lai. I am a Mende man from a Mende country in Africa, Sa Lone . . .

SENGBE: *(Curiously.)* You speak Arabic?

SA: Yes. I speak and write Arabic. I can read Koran.

SENGBE: Hhnn . . . where did they capture you?

SA: On the road to Charang—in Bandi country. My uncle buy two slave of Bandi to give as payment of old, old debt. One slave ran away . . .

SENGBE: So the creditors seize you?

SA: Yes.

KIMBO: My own king sell me in Bullom country. Blacksmith, me . . . first blacksmith in Bullom country to sell for slave.

GABRO: Enemies surround my village. After big fight, they capture me and sell me to Senor . . .

FULLEH: That is my son. *(Indicating* Gabro.*)*

SENGBE: Where are you from?

FULLEH: From Temne country. Me—hunter. I kills five elephant, sis alligator. Bum-bam-bum-bam.

OTHERS: *(Impressed.)* Hhnnn!

SESSI: Look at me. I am Bandi. When slave men attack me, there was big fight. Slave men shoot me in leg. *(Showing his scars.)* Look. See? They shoot me in leg before they able to capture me.

OTHERS: Hhnnn . . .

SENGBE: (*To* Kale.) Boy, what is your name?

KALE: My name is Kale.

SENGBE: Boy Kale, what happened to you?

KALE: I was captured in the bush near my house.

KAGNE: (*The eldest of the three girls.*) Me and my sisters were sold by our stepfather to pay a debt . . .

There is an outburst of laughter which ends the conversation. The lights turn on. Montez *and* Reira *seem to be celebrating after their satisfying trade deals.*

RUIZ: (*Holding* Montez *by the shoulder.*) Senor Pedro Montez, my brother, we can travel together—if you don't mind. You do not need to hire another vessel. I have already hired *La Amistad*. After all, we are all going to Puerto Principe. Unless you have your travel plans made, what do you say? Are you travelling with us?

MONTEZ: Of course I will travel with you, Pepe. The more, the merrier. Is that not so, Senor Reira? (*Laughter again.*)

RUIZ: (*Excitedly, calling out.*) Antonio!! Antonio!!

ANTONIO: (*Dashing in.*) Si . . . Senor Pepe. Everything is ready.

RUIZ: Make room for Senor Pedro Montez. He is transporting his cargo with us. Make room for the four children—three girls and one boy. We leave now. We have a long march to make through the jungle—the whole night. You know that.

ANTONIO: We are ready, Senor. We can leave now. (*With his whip raised high, registering lashes from time to time to the* Slaves.) Move!! (*As the* Slaves, *in their despondent mood break into an African dirge, the men embrace and bid farewell.*)

REIRA: Goodbye, Pepe. Goodbye, Pedro. Adios. We will see each other again. Anytime you want to bargain for your family estates, don't forget to come to me.

RUIZ: Adios, amigo. I will not forget you.

MONTEZ: Adios, Senor Reira. We will see again.

REIRA: And gentlemen, don't forget. From now on your cargoes are ladinos—born in Cuba, not Africans just arriving here. You got it? La-di-nos!

MEN: (*In chorus.*) La-di-nos!

ANTONIO: (*Breaks in for final take-off.*) Mmooooovvee!!

Blackout. As the whip registers again and the exodus begins, the dirge decreases and fades far into the night with sounds of occasional cries, whip cracks, and curses. A spotlight soon focuses on Sengbe—being the last in line. He is flanked by Ruiz and Antonio, who stands with his whip raised high over Sengbe, threateningly. All are in freeze.

SENGBE: (*Narratively.*) My dear people. You haven't seen anything yet. You haven't heard anything yet. My story is only just beginning. (*Pause.*) You see how I was captured by those men. How my right hand was tied to my neck and I was dragged away. Well, the men who captured me, took me to a man called Mayagilalo—who sent them. Mayagilalo gave me over to King Mana Shaka—the Vai king—in settlement of a debt. After staying in Shaka's town for a month, I was marched back to Lomboko—a notorious slave trading island near Sulima, on the Gallinas coast—and sold to the richest slave dealer there—the Spaniard, Pedro Blanco. In Lomboko, I was imprisoned with other slaves while fresh ones continued to join us—for two months. Most of the captives came from Mende country, but others were Kono, Sherbro, Temne, Kissi, and Gbandi. Most of us spoke Mende and were farmers. Others were hunters and blacksmiths. After two months in Lomboko, we were all shipped across the Atlantic—in March. We were over four hundred, on board, when we reached Havana—the Spanish colony of Cuba—in 1839. We were, then, put at a slave auction. Jose Ruiz bought me and forty-eight others, as you can see. Pedro Montez has bought four children—three girls and a boy. We are now all bound for Puerto Principe—fifty-three of us. And you know what? From my discovery, we all—the fifty-three captives—happen to be Sa Lone people. And we all speak Mende.

Blackout. As the whips register again, the cries and curses blend with the dirge which increases again and fades into the stillness of the night.

Amistad Kata-Kata

SCENE FOUR

Inside La Amistad—*a small and sleek black schooner. Night—with only a faint glow of light, focusing on* Captain Ramon Ferrer—*the owner. Ferrer and the two Spaniards are seen preparing for a routine trip. Sounds of rough winds and waves breaking against the vessel, fill the background.*

CAPTAIN: (*Calling out.*) Antonio!! Antonio!!

ANTONIO: (*Hurries in.*) Yeees Capitan!!

CAPTAIN: Are we ready for the journey? All fifty-three slaves on board?

ANTONIO: All fifty-three slaves on board, Capitan. They are down below deck. The two owners said that we must chain them together and this what I have done.

CAPTAIN: Good. The two sailors ready?

ANTONIO: The two sailors are ready, Capitan. They are down below—lowering the sails. They say a big storm is on the way.

CAPTAIN: Where is Celestino?

ANTONIO: He is down below—cooking for dinner. Food will be ready soon.

CAPTAIN: Antonio, tell Celestino we will be hungry soon. (*Antonio hurries out.*)

RUIZ: Capitan Ferrer, I don't think it will take us three nights and two days to reach Puerto Principe. The winds are adverse.

CAPTAIN: Yeah . . . the weather is not good enough . . .

MONTEZ: True. The winds are adverse. Unless the winds change, it will take more than three nights and two days to reach Puerto Principe . . .

RUIZ: . . . And do we not have enough supplies to last more than two days and three nights?

CAPTAIN: We'll have to reduce the slaves' ration of food and water, immediately. Celestino!!! Celestino!!! Where is Celestino?!!!

CELESTINO: (*Rushes in.*) Siii . . . Capitannnn!!

CAPTAIN: Celestino, reduce the slaves' ration of food and water, immediately. The two slave owners have chartered the trip to Puerto Principe and it is our responsibility to reach them there, without any further charge. From now on: one banana, two potatoes, and small cup of water per day for each black. Allow a few of the blacks at a time to exercise on deck.

CELESTINO: (*Sensing danger, attempts to protest.*) Ah! Capitan that can be dangerous. In case there is trouble . . .

CAPTAIN: Celestino.

CELESTINO: Si, Capitan.

CAPTAIN: Go.

>Celestino *leaves hesitantly. Complete silence fills the air as they are well aware of their risky actions.* Celestino *reenters with food and serves. They start eating and* Montez *breaks the silence.*

MONTEZ: This journey is going to be long and hard. I can already feel it. We must be careful.

RUIZ: What's the matter, Pedro?

Captain: What's up, Pedro? Everything is all right.

MONTEZ: Everything is not alright. I was a sea captain myself. Reducing the slaves' rations can bring trouble. When there is trouble, slave owners forfeit their property. Sometimes, slave owners die.

RUIZ: Don't say that, Senor Montez. This ship is carrying a lot of cargo, right now, in this journey—fifty-three slaves, plus other cargo and provisions worth forty-thousand dollars: dishes, cloth, jewelry, luxury items . . .

CELESTINO: (*Suddenly crashing in.*) Capitan!!! Capitan!!! The slave!! The black!!

CAPTAIN: What's the matter, Celestino, what's wrong?

ANTONIO: It is the slave, Lopez. You said, cut down on food and water. I cut down on food and water. You say, take slave out and exercise on deck. I take slave out and exercise. Now, Lopez steal water. Lopez, the black, steal water.

Amistad Kata-Kata

Lights focus on Slaves *being exercised on the deck by* Antonio *and the two* Sailors. *The* Slave *who stole water being man-handled on the floor.* Ruiz *enters, furious.*

RUIZ: For stealing water and drinking more than allotted—sixty lashes! (*The other slaves watch the wounds inflicted all over the body of the battered* Slave.) Good. This is a lesson to all of you. As long as you are my property—no stealing. Okay? Now, apply the sailors' medicine on those wounds. (*Immediately,* Antonio *fetches a jar containing the mixture and opens it. Before he applies—*Ruiz *threatens.*) You see this mixture, negro fellows. It's for you. For the wounds and cuts after we beat you, when you steal—water, anything.

The mixture is applied. The Slave *screams as loud as he can. His companions cry with him and feel the pain with him.* Ruiz, *feeling satisfied with his action, bursts into laughter as he exits.* Antonio *and the* Sailors, *sensing the atmosphere, slip out, leaving the* Slaves *by themselves. They whimper, moan, and curse.* Celestino *returns, after clearing the dishes, on his way to the kitchen.* Sengbe *becomes increasingly restless, in his concern over the Spaniards' intentions. He corners* Celestino, *to talk to him.*

SENGBE: What is the white man going to do to us?

CELESTINO: (*In a cruel jest, grinning.*) Upon arrival in Puerto Principe, (*indicating with his fingers*) the Spaniards plan to kill you, chop you up into pieces, dry you up, and eat you.

He bursts out laughing and hurries out. Sengbe *and his companions are stunned by* Celestino's *revelation.* Sengbe *is furious with himself. On this third night at sea,* Sengbe *works closely with his companions to mount an insurrection.*

SENGBE: My brothers, this is our third night on this ship. We have just learned that the white man is going to eat us. We don't know where they are taking us to be eaten. The wind, as you can see, is very strong. I am sure that we are going to be at sea much longer than we expect.

GABRO: It's true, Sengbe. You are right.

OTHERS: (*Variously.*) It's true. You are right. The wind is very strong. The white men want to eat us.

SENGBE: (*Throwing the bait.*) It is possible for us to return to Africa.

OTHERS: (*Variously.*) Hhnnn!! What? You say what? Impossible!! How? Tell us how!! (*Mixed feelings.*) You are right. That is in the hands of God. We are in trouble already. Are you mad? Let us leave trouble alone. What is wrong with him, for God's sake? Perhaps I am dreaming...

SENGBE: (*Tactfully.*) Yes, if we want to, we can return home again.

GABRO: Perhaps, you know how. You just tell us how. (*Silence.*)

SENGBE: You all know that we have been sailing in the direction of the setting sun, since we left Africa.

KIMBO: Yes. We all know that. How to return? You just tell us.

SENGBE: So, by sailing in the opposite direction—there lies our home.

KIMBO: (*Becoming impatient.*) How? We only want to know how.

SENGBE: (*Senses support, becomes more and more tactful.*) Well... you see... there are fifty-three of us on board...

GABRO: That is including the four children.

SENGBE: Yes. There are fifty-three of us against only seven of them—including the two slaves of the Captain.

GABRO: That is Antonio and Celestino.

SENGBE: Yes.

KIMBO: Okay. We are fifty-three and they are seven. So what?

SENGBE: So, we may as well die trying to free ourselves than to be killed and eaten. (*Sends shock waves. Fear aroused. Tension builds.*) As for me—I am ready. Whether you join me or not, I am ready to fight the white man—single-handed. I was not born to be a slave—let alone be killed and eaten.

Silence again. Deep thought.

Amistad Kata-Kata

GABRO: *(Breaking the silence.)* You are right, Sengbe. Death is death. Whether we are killed and eaten or we are slain in battle—it is the same death. It is for us, now, to choose an honorable death.

KIMBO: So it is better to die fighting . . .

SENGBE: . . . than to be killed and eaten.

Another silence.

JASABE: But, we are all chained. Our hands and necks are chained.

OTHERS: *(Variously.)* Yes. We are all chained. We can't do anything. I am there to . . . when trouble will come. Who among us is not chained?

SENGBE: Okay. Listen. As were being exercised on deck three days ago, I found a loose spike which I used, secretly, to break my chains.

Reveals free hands.

OTHERS: *(Variously. Wonder, shock, disbelief.)* Sengbe, O Sengbe, you are a man. Untie us. I guarantee you, Sengbe . . . No wonder you were so quiet these days . . . busy untying yourself. Free us, Sengbe. Free us—we are brothers. You are a man, Sengbe. This is our chance, Sengbe. Our chance to be free. Untie us now. Now, before it is too late.

SENGBE: Wait—all of you. Not yet. We still have to pretend and plan properly. We must not miss. *(To the boy.)* Kale, you will stay here and take care of the other children.

JASABE: Kale, did you hear? That is your own to do.

GABRO: Sengbe, tell us what to do, because the Captain is armed with pistols and cutlass. We are not.

KIMBO: Yes. They are all armed. The masters are armed with pistols and crewmen with cutlasses. We are not.

SENGBE: Okay. Listen. On the way to deck, inside the cargo by the steps, I saw several daggers—terrible, strong, machete type with wide, bloodthirsty blades, suitable for chopping heads. *(Senses support, pauses.)* I will untie you. Those fit for the battle will come with me. I will lead you.

OTHERS: *(Determined.)* We are ready!!!

SENGBE: *(Pleased.)* I am happy. Your renewed strength has suddenly intensified my courage and will power to fight the white man to the last tooth. But first, we must swear.

GABRO: Yes, we must swear. All men must swear, whether you come with us or not.

SENGBE: *(Taking water from the bucket.)* Everybody, including the children, place your hand on this cup and repeat after me. *(All obey.)* I swear that I will never surrender to the white man. None of us will be left in slavery. We rather die fighting. God be with us. Now, one after the other, let us drink.

Sengbe drinks first and passes. The sacrament goes around. Suddenly, footsteps are heard off-stage. Antonio *enters and looks around. All quiet. He cross-checks and raises his whip threateningly. Feeling satisfied, he leaves. Blackout on Slaves. Lights come up on* Captain *and the two Spaniards on deck. They look worried.*

MONTEZ: Captain, tempers are raising among the blacks. A few moments ago, one sailor heard some of the blacks noisily coming up the hold towards the forecastle, but ordered them back below.

RUIZ: See, the winds are shifting. There is going to be another storm.

CAPTAIN: True. There is going to be another storm. We cannot make any trip ashore for more provisions. *(Calls out.)* Antonio!! Antonio!! Where is Antonio?!

ANTONIO: *(Hurries in.)* Si . . . Capitan!!!

CAPTAIN: Where were you, Antonio? Where were you?

ANTONIO: I went down below to see how things are with the slaves.

CAPTAIN: How are things with the slaves, Antonio?

Enter Celestino.

ANTONIO: They are calm, Captain, Do not worry.

CAPTAIN: Antonio, Celestino, I am worried. We have spent too long on this journey. With the slaves' rations cut down so dramatically, it can be dangerous, Antonio. I cannot run into port, now, for supplies because that means additional expense for me. The two slave owners have contracted the trip to Puerto Principe and it is my responsibility to get them there without any further charge. I am worried . . .

CELESTINO: Do not worry, Capitan. The slaves are calm. There will be no trouble. The Africans are quite content . . .

Suddenly, a loud noise and the scuffle of many feet on the deck, followed by screams of "murder." Jumping from their bunks, the two Spaniards and the two Sailors rush toward the sound of the noise. They are face to face with the Slaves who emerged from their hold, led by Sengbe. Before the whites could reach for their pistols, the Slaves, armed with cutlasses, swords, knives, and sticks, have, in a few moments, gained the deck. As the Slaves close in, the Captain, wielding his sword, yells out to Celestino.

CAPTAIN: (*In desperation.*) Celestino!! Throw some bread at them!! Celestino!! Bread!!

The Africans ignore the basket of bread at their feet. With his heavy, steel blade, Sengbe strikes Celestino to the floor, leaving the others to strangle him to death. The Captain kills one of his assailants and injures two others. Again, Sengbe's sword strikes the Captain dead. Ruiz and Montez try to regain control. Pedro draws out a knife, slashes a few of them, and tries to frighten them and break the mutiny. But the sight of their blood drives the Africans into a frenzy. Montez receives a hard blow to his head with a cane knife, which knocks him senseless to the floor. As the unequal battle rages on, with two Africans killed and a few others wounded, the two Sailors cut themselves loose and jump overboard. Two Africans chase but are too late to stop them. Curses of, "You bastards! Man-eating motherfuckers! Why don't you wait? Come back here!" can be heard from back stage. Unnoticed and witnessing Celestino's murder, Antonio has hid. Crawling through the darkness, he squeezes behind a food barrel and pulls an old sail over himself. Sengbe Pieh and the others overpower Ruiz who is also bleeding and now sits on the floor with his hands tied. Only dimly conscious, Montez is dragged on deck with his hands tied. Sengbe and the others tie one of

Ruiz's hands to one of Montez's. Sengbe *raises his sword, ready to bury it in the* Spaniard's *body. The two men scream and beg for their lives while trying to escape the rain of blows, but before* Sengbe *inflicts the mortal wound,* Gabro *grabs his hand.*

SENGBE: We are going to kill all of the white men.

GABRO: No, Sengbe. Alone, we cannot sail the ship back to Africa. Let us save the white men and the cabin boy, Antonio.

At this juncture, they notice the absence of Antonio.

SENGBE: Where is Antonio?

Angrily, some of the Africans *go searching in the pale light.* Antonio *attempts to lie still but he is breathing heavily and shaking uncontrollably. Suddenly, his cover is thrown off.* Antonio *screams and begs for mercy. He is dragged back, where he realizes that the lives of* Ruiz *and* Montez *are also spared.*

BONA: It's true, Sengbe. Let's save Antonio. He is our only contact with the white men. He can speak Spanish and understand us better.

The others concur and support him.

SENGBE: Okay. All right. (*Suddenly,* Ruiz *attempts to escape. Five slaves dash after him, hustle him, kicking and spitting at him.*) Now listen everyone. We are taking these two men to the helm to turn the ship and sail us back to Africa. (*To the* Spaniards.) You will, most certainly, be killed if you don't get us back to Africa. During our journey from Africa to Cuba, we sailed away from the rising sun. So, to return, you must take the *Amistad* into the sun. Go. (*Pointing east.*). Head straight for the rising sun. That is our way home.

BONA: And if any of you try to escape, we will kill you.

At the helm, under Sengbe's *instruction, they loosen the two men's bonds. Then the* Africans *take off their blood covered clothes, use the keys to the trunks, find new clothes, and put them on. Three strong men are set to guard* them. *The whites are now in a sorry state. They gaze around at the remains of the mutiny.*

MONTEZ: (*Whispering in Spanish so that the guards do not understand.*) Pepe, I have devised a plan whereby I would, during the day, steer the vessel eastward in the proper direction but, at night, turn northward, and they would not know. They can tell only by the sun, and there is no sun at night.

RUIZ: That's a good idea. Perhaps we would be rescued.

The remaining slaves, who did not take part in the mutiny, emerge from different corners—jubilantly singing and dancing, but Sengbe is quick to call their attention.

SENGBE: Listen everyone. (*Silence.*) As you can see, we have taken command of the ship. Captain Ferrer and his cook, Celestino, are dead. Montez and Ruiz have surrendered—after sustaining several mild wounds. They will sail us back home, to Africa. Antonio will be needed for our return journey, so he is spared—tied to the anchor. The two sailors have disappeared—probably drowned after jumping overboard and trying to swim. In just a few minutes, the mutiny has succeeded. (*Cheers, bursting into singing and dancing in praise of Sengbe. After a few minutes,* Sengbe *calms them down again.*) All right . . . all right . . . okay . . . listen. (*Silence.*) You see . . . we are only just beginning our struggle to regain our freedom. This ship is not Africa, and until we get home, we are not free. We will take these men to the helm to see that they sail us back to Africa. They will, most certainly, be killed if they don't get us back. Meanwhile, drag the bodies of the captain and cook to the side, throw them overboard, and let's start cleaning up and getting ready for our return journey.

The Africans *drag the bodies of* Ferrer *and* Celestino *to the side and throw them overboard. They wash down the deck—stained red, with blood. A ghostly silence, usually accompanying death, prevails over the eerie sound of creaking mast and sail rustling in the breeze. Suddenly, the* Africans *break the casks of beef and water, and satisfy themselves. They continue to emerge, carrying boxes and bottles. They find jewelry, dresses, and shoes, which they put on. Overexcited, they eat from the boxes and drink from the bottles. Soon, many become drunk or sick. Then* Sengbe *reappears, dressed in white pantaloons and a red scarf around his neck. He has a pistol in his left hand and a sword in his right.* Sengbe *picks up a dance and the rest join in celebration. Blackout on* Africans. *Music and noise fade into the night. After a few moments, a spotlight focuses on* Sengbe *as he continues his narrative.*

Sengbe: (*Solemnly addressing the audience.*) My dear people, thus began the strangest voyage that has ever sailed on the seven seas. Two months passed and we were still at sea. A three day journey has taken two months. By this time my companions were terrified at the thought of dying at sea. Food and water were running out (*Light comes on deck, as* Sengbe *continues his narrative, revealing the gloomy situation aboard.*) Everyone was starving to death. Some of my companions, dehydrated from thirst, drank liquids from bottles only to become sick and die from medicines and other poisonous substances. Gloom and despair cast a heavy shadow on us—the Amistads. So far, nine of my companions were dead. Ruiz, Montez, and Antonio were also in a sorry state—out of food and water. They were also begging to drink salt water, which made them, also, sick. I did not trust them. I did not trust them at all. Their actions throughout the journey had been very suspicious. They were up to something. So, as usual, I summoned my strong men to a brief meeting. (*Suddenly, his mood changes to "no nonsense" as he summons his strongmen around him.*) Gabro, Kai, Jasabe, Sa, Kimbo, Fulleh . . . (*They assemble around him.*) . . . this time we are going to kill the white men. Immediately!! (*He dashes toward* Montez *with a dagger but is held back by some who still disagree.* Montez *immediately falls to his knees, begging for mercy.*) Look here. Pedro is fooling us into believing that he is sailing the vessel towards Africa.

Gabro: You are right, Sengbe. I have also noticed. At night, Montez seems to be turning the vessel to Havana.

Sengbe: To further obstruct the voyage, he keeps the sails flapping in the wind—causing the vessel to move very slowly, during the day.

Kimbo: In fact, right now we are nowhere near Africa.

Amistad Kata-Kata

GABRO: We don't even know where we are heading.

SENGBE: But it is better to remain in this ship and die in the open sea than to be made slaves again. (*Suddenly, one African begins to choke and cry out. Sengbe and others rush to his aid. They struggle to save his life but he dies.*) That is it. One more brother dead. Ten of us are now dead. It is possible that more of us will die.

JASABE: Can't we put up at a nearby island and get food and water?

KIMBO: No, no. That can be dangerous. We could be captured and enslaved again. We have sworn.

KAI: I agree with Kimbo. We do not know which of these islands are slave islands. Let us continue.

OTHERS: (*Concurring, variously.*) Yes. Let us continue. It can be dangerous. We have sworn.

SENGBE: Okay. If the conditions onboard the ship become worse, we will have no choice but to order the ship close to shore. I will go with Gabro and Kimbo . . .

KAI: (*Volunteering.*) . . . and me!

SENGBE: . . . Okay, and Kai, to buy food and water.

KIMBO: What will we use to buy, Sengbe?

SENGBE: There are a lot of gold doubloons on this ship. We will buy with them. Meanwhile, from now on, we are going to double our precautions. Nothing must be eaten but what I hand out. No one but the children will receive a full ration of food and water from now on. (*Blackout. Spotlight on* Sengbe—*his narrative continues.*) We began to encounter other vessels. First, a pilot boat came alongside our ship. I immediately sent the two white men below so they could not be seen. I used Antonio to make it clear to them that we needed food and water. They passed over bread and water, which we devoured. We learned from the captain that we were now in the waters of North America. So, we were right. Montez and Ruiz had tricked us. We were nowhere near Africa. They had to die, now. Suddenly, this pilot ship began to tow our ship to where, I don't know. "To safety," Antonio told us. "To what safety?" I flared. Suddenly (*mimicking*) my companions and I attempted jumping into the pilot ship. Seeing our knives and swords, the master cut off the tow rope and fled. Several other sea captains sighted us but hastily departed as soon as they saw a large number of blacks armed with knives and dressed in alien costumes, looking desperate. By late 1839, the *Amistad* had caused considerable stir along the North American coast.

Blackout.

SCENE FIVE

Office of the Comptroller—New York harbor. Early September, 1839. The Comptroller walks in with his briefcase and some of the day's newspapers, which he puts on the desk, as he tries to settle down. Suddenly, 1st Captain dashes in.

1st Captain: *(Terror-stricken.)* Mr. Comptroller, Sir, there is danger along the east coast, Sir.

Comptroller: What do you mean, Captain?

1st Captain: There is a long, low, black schooner zig-zagging up the eastern coast. And the people of Green Port, East Harbor, and New London are in grave danger. We happened to spot the ship, so we drew near to examine this strange, almost derelict schooner. As we came alongside, we saw that there were about twenty-five to thirty blacks on board. I suspect that the ship is a slaver, whose slaves had risen and probably murdered the captain and crew.

2nd Captain: *(Rushing in, horrified.)* Mr. Comptroller, Sir, a grave news, Sir. There is foul play and piracy along our eastern coast, Sir. On my way from Norfolk, I spotted a low, black schooner thirty-five miles off Egg Harbor . . .

1st Captain: . . . Thank you, Captain. As if I were lying . . .

Comptroller: *(Stupefied.)* Let him continue, Captain.

2nd Captain: Eh . . . the sails are tatters. It is flying only the fore-top sail and the bottom is painted green and in terrible condition. From my observation, the blacks in it are out of water and have been drinking salt water for several days now.

Comptroller: Did you also happen to enter the schooner?

2nd Captain: Yes, I did—and found twenty-five persons on deck and a large number in the hold—apparently in a state of starvation, all black men—none of whom could speak English.

1st Captain: Did you, at all, attempt to take the schooner in tow, Captain?

2nd Captain: I did, but was lucky to notice the ring leader carrying a pistol and a sword, making preparation to capture my ship. Sensing the threat, I cast off the tow—losing my line but saving my ship and crew of seven.

Enter Lieutenant Gedney, U.S. Naval officer.

Lt. Gedney: *(Calm.)* Hello, gentlemen.

Others: Hello, Lieutenant

Lt. Gedney: Gentlemen, are you aware of the problem?

Comptroller: Yes, of course, Lieutenant. I was just thinking of going over to your office. Eh . . . can it be true?

Lt. Gedney: That is why I am here. True or not—we are not going to take any chances. Right now, the United States government has ordered the U.S. Surveying Brigade *Washington*, under my command, to survey the entire north eastern seaboard to find and capture the *Amistad*.

Comptroller: The *Amistad*?

Lt. Gedney: That's the name of the mysterious schooner. Captain Sears has just left and gone home. We were together in Lieutenant Meade's office. Captain Sears's ship has just encountered the *Amistad* while traveling from Bedford to Wilmington. He said that he boarded the ship and found the deck littered with broken glasses and other remains of cargo. He was told that the ship had been out about three months. Captain Sears also saw white men onboard.

Others: *(Shocked.)* White men onboard?

LT. GEDNEY: Yes. He said that they even took the *Amistad* in tow until it was quite dark when he heard a voice, in English, tell the blacks to make sail, get alongside his own ship, the *Emeline*, and capture food and water. So, Captain Sears became frightened and cut off . . .

Suddenly, the voices off anti-Amistad protesters are heard offstage. The men listen carefully as they move towards the entrance, making it possible for them to "see" the crowd, while the audience still does not.

CROWD (*Variously.*) Stop the pirates!! Capture the cannibals!! Save the white race!! Down with savagery!! We are not safe!! Our life is threatened!! We can't sail our own ships!! We can't go fishing!!...

COMPTROLLER: Okay . . . all right . . . listen everybody . . .

Fails to calm the crowd.

1ST CAPTAIN: (*Helping with crowd.*) Thank you . . . thank you. Please allow the Comptroller to speak. (Lt. Gedney *exits.*) Okay . . . the Comptroller has good news for us. Let us give him a chance. (*Noise subsides.*) Thank you. Thank you very much.

COMPTROLLER: Thank you. Thank you all very much for expressing your concern. I assure you that the authorities are quite aware of the presence of the long, low, black schooner that has appeared on our north eastern coast and are taking all possible steps to remedy the situation. (*Mixed reaction from demonstrators.*) And right now, as I speak, the United States government has ordered the U.S. Surveying Brigade, commanded by Lt. Commander Gedney, who has just left, to survey the entire eastern coast, to find and capture the *Amistad*.

Cheers and sounds of mixed responses from crowd. Blackout.

SCENE SIX

The Amistad, with the United States Naval contingent led by Lt. Meade, already onboard. As Sengbe *is away, the* Africans *put up no resistance. Their faces are of mingled curiosity and fear. All about the deck is evidence of wasteful destruction.* With the blacks under control, the Americans search and find Ruiz and Montez and release them from the guards that the Africans had posted. As soon as they are released, the whites waste no time in making their plight known.

RUIZ: (*Recovering from shock.*) These negroes are our slaves. They have risen and taken the vessel.

MONTEZ: This ship, *La Amistad*, is a Spanish slave ship, registered to transport fifty-three ladinos, as slaves, belonging to us, from Havana to Puerto Principe. This ship and this slave (*indicating* Antonio) belong to the slain Capitan Ferrer . . .

RUIZ: All items on this ship are our property . . . That is the leader!

Ruiz points to Sengbe, *who is led in by the* Lt. Commander, *manacled with his strongmen, carrying a sack and some other items.* Sengbe *wears a red flannel shirt and duck pantaloons, with a scarf around his neck, holding a snuffbox, seemingly calm and in control. At first, smiling, showing hand motions that he expected to be hanged, he then turns and stares intensely at* Montez *and* Ruiz, *who take shelter behind the* Americans. *On* Sengbe's *entry, the* Americans *go on full alert—pointing their guns and giving commands which* Sengbe *tends to ignore. Once on deck, it is obvious who the leader of the* Africans *is. They cheer and embrace* Sengbe *and are no longer as timid as before.*

SENGBE: My dear people, we would have returned but the gods are against us. We headed ashore for provisions and we managed to purchase two dogs, which we have already slaughtered; some sweet potatoes; and a bottle of gin with the Spanish gold doubloons. Two white captains had even offered to sail us back to Sierra Leone if we paid them in gold doubloons. I had planned to get the journey under way in the morning. Indeed, we could have returned. Now, I think that I will be killed. But that does not pain me, if by dying, that would save my people from the bondage of the white man, forever. So, let us fight to the death rather than surrender.

Officers immediately grab Sengbe *at gun point and handcuff him with the others.*

LT. GEDNEY: As far as we are concerned, you Africans are slaves, mutineers, and murderers. You have captured a man's ship, killed the captain and cook, imprisoned your owner, and tried to sail away to Africa. This is a clear case of piracy and murder on the high seas. Move!!

The Africans break into a dirge as they are led away. Blackout.

SCENE SEVEN

On the bush path—returning after the ceremony. When light comes on, Grandma's laughter precedes their entry. Grandma is hunch-backed, uses a walking stick, chews kola nuts, and smokes a pipe.

GRANDMA: *(Deep in laughter.)* . . . Ta . . . faylay . . . sawa . . . nani . . . lolu . . . that's all? That's all this man did?

STUDENT: Yes, Grandma. They needed an interpreter badly—who could speak Mende and record their own version of the revolt.

GRANDMA: So, this man . . . this church man . . . eh . . .

STUDENT: Professor Gibbs.

GRANDMA: Yes . . . Professor Gibbs. He volunteered.

STUDENT: . . . Yes . . . to find an interpreter.

GRANDMA: So he learned to count from one to ten in Mende and then went to the ports—counting to all the African sailors he met. *(Laughter again.)* Ta . . . faylay . . . sawa . . . nani . . . lolu . . . that is very funny. That is the funniest thing that came out of Sengbe's mouth.

STUDENT: But, it worked, Grandma. It paid. He discovered someone.

GRANDMA: I know, but it's funny. *(To the audience.)* My people, isn't it funny—what the churchman did?

STUDENT: *(Also to audience.)* People, please don't mind Grandma. Professor Gibbs found a man called James Covey—a seaman, on a British warship. Covey, a Mende man, had been captured and sold as a child, but was re-captured by British squadrons and taken to

Amistad Kata-Kata

Sierra Leone, where he was released. He learned to speak English, fluently, and joined the British navy. People, can you imagine how the captives jumped and shouted for joy when they heard Covey speak their language?

GRANDMA: *(On a serious note.)* I know . . .

STUDENT: So, that was how the captives were able to tell the full version of their own side of the events.

GRANDMA: Sengbe is a very good story teller. Throughout his narrative, everyone was spellbound. By the time the ceremony had ended, the whole story was unfolded. Now we know how he was captured and sold into slavery . . .

STUDENT: . . . and how he fought for his freedom and won. But Grandma, these people still don't know everything yet. And that is why they are here.

GRANDMA: So, they must know. Let's share with them.

STUDENT: You don't mind, Grandma?

GRANDMA: No. Let's share together. That's why we are here. Son, let's start with their arrival in America.

STUDENT: Okay. *(Referring to his notes, intermittently.)* According to Sengbe, one week after their arrival in the United States, an abolitionist group formed to defend them. This committee became known as the "Amistad Committee"—Sengbe and his companions, the "Amistad" captives.

GRANDMA: Interesting. Do you remember Sengbe saying that the committee was not happy with the treatment that they received?

STUDENT: Yes. The Americans immediately released Ruiz and Montez and ordered that Sengbe and his companions were put in jail—awaiting trial for murder and piracy.

GRANDMA: Stupid!! Murder, my foot!! I wish I was there.

STUDENT: What would you have done, Grandma?

GRANDMA: What would I have done? I would have come down hard on the Americans. I would have hit them hard with my walking stick. As for Ruiz and Montez—they are disgusting. They changed Sengbe Pieh's name to . . . to . . . eh . . .

STUDENT: Jose Cinqué.

GRANDMA: Look at that. A Spanish name. Who would hear that name and think that he was African . . . That is why he was so entirely forgotten by his people.

STUDENT: A great tragedy, Grandma.

GRANDMA: Tragedy, indeed. It makes me quiver. Ah . . . son, give me my bag. Let me have a taste of my ground kola nut. Your Grandma no longer has teeth to chew the nut. (Student *helps* Grandma *to her kola.*) Thank you very much, my son.

STUDENT: It's a pleasure, Grandma.

GRANDMA: Let's come to the story, again. The people here are anxious to know. Okay. Where were we?

STUDENT: The Amistad Committee.

GRANDMA: Yes. The Amistad Committee. What next?

STUDENT: (*Flashback on three men as they are introduced one by one. Seems a meeting place for an appointment, on the other end of the stage.*) Well . . . the Amistad Committee was comprised of, among many others, a man named Louis Tappan, a wealthy New York merchant, strong church figure, and prominent abolitionist famous in the United States at that time because he was violently opposed to slavery; Joshua Leavitt, editor of an American anti-slavery magazine; and Reverend Simeon Joselyn, a white pastor of a black church.

GRANDMA: Yes, it was they who went to find a good lawyer to defend the Africans in the high court.

STUDENT: Yes. Even though they had won in the lower court, the committee had to work out a defense strategy to ensure that the verdict did not go against them, now. They searched for a public figure of the highest standing to plead the case of the Amistad captives before the United States Supreme Court.

GRANDMA: So, that was how they persuaded the former United States president . . .

STUDENT: . . . John Quincy Adams to lead the defense.

Light focuses on the three men, as blackout falls on Grandma *and* Student. *The three gentlemen knock on the door of* John Quincy Adams, *who opens and lets the visitors in.*

SCENE EIGHT

The living room of John Quincy Adams—*former President of the United States—March, 1840. When the lights come on, the three visitors are knocking on Adams's door. Adams, who was reading, opens the door and lets them in. They exchange greetings and make introductions. They take off their coats and hang them. As the meeting progresses,* Adams's *chef serves drinks, coffee, and snacks.*

ADAMS: Now gentlemen, what can I do for you?

TAPPAN: Thirty-eight yellow men from Africa, have been piratically kidnapped from their native land, transported across the seas, subjected to atrocious cruelties, and have been thrown upon our shores. They are now incarcerated—in jail to await their trial for crimes alleged to have been committed by them.

SIMEON: They are ignorant of our language—of the uses of civilized society and the obligations of Christianity.

TAPPAN: It is under these circumstances that several friends of human rights and abolition of the slave trade have met to consult upon the case of these unfortunate Africans and appointed a committee to employ all the necessary means to secure the rights of the accused.

LEAVITT: The committee is currently employing three legal gentlemen of distinguished ability as defense counsel.

ADAMS: And who are these three distinguished gentlemen?

LEAVITT: Roger Baldwin, Seth Staples, and Theodore Sedgwick—among the best minds of the day. The committee has also been fortunate enough to find an interpreter. The best . . .

ADAMS: An American?

LEAVITT: No sir. An African. A Sierra Leonean, in fact. A native of the very home of the captives. He happens to be a sailor on the British warship, *Buzzard*.

ADAMS: What are the views of the President of the United States, Martin Van Buren, on the question of this affair?

TAPPAN: Well . . . since he depends on the support of the southern, pro-slavery democrats for next year's presidential election, Van Buren is hoping that the court will order the captives returned to Cuba, thus relieving him of political pressure from both the southern democrats and the Spanish government.

LEAVITT: In fact, he has declared that the Africans are to be considered the property of those for whom the Spanish Consul is claiming, and that the ship should be returned, with all its contents, to Cuba.

TAPPAN: And the cabinet endorses that view. So, you see, Sir, our committee has realized that on the basis of law and argument, we would have a hard time convincing the Supreme Court to release the Amistad captives. We have, therefore, decided to get a very good lawyer, with a great deal of prestige . . .

SIMEON: . . . yes, a person the court could not ignore as a man, even if they could ignore his argument.

ADAMS: (*Startled.*) But I am seventy-three years old, physically weak and feeble, and have not argued a case in the United States Supreme Court for over thirty years, now.

SIMEON: But you are a renowned lawyer, Sir—a current Congressman and former President of the United States. Our committee has the utmost faith in you that, in the name of humanity and justice and by the power of the almighty God, you will succeed.

LEAVITT: The situation, as we now approach the *Amistad*, Sir, is a dangerous one for us. Though we have won in the lower courts, the judges in the Supreme Court are biased towards pro-slavery interests. There are a bunch of southern judges in the Supreme Court. The situation is dangerous for us, Sir.

TAPPAN: We want to see if a man, although he is black, cannot have justice done him here in the United States of America.

Suddenly, a knock at the door.

LEAVITT: I'll get it.

Leavitt goes to door and opens it—surprised but happy to receive Sengbe and Kale. Greetings and courtesies.

TAPPAN: *(Making introductions.)* Mr. Adams, Sir, these are the heroes of the *Amistad* revolt. This is Joseph Cinqué . . .

SENGBE: . . . Sengbe Pieh.

TAPPAN: Sorry. This is Sengbe Pieh—the leader who has become a public figure in the United States, and many are anxious to see the man whom the northern newspapers compared to the heroes of ancient Greece and Rome. He is also known as the "Black Prince."

SENGBE: Good evening, Mr. Adams.

ADAMS: *(Shaking hands.)* Good evening. You are doing so well. Keep it up.

TAPPAN: And this is little Kale.

KALE: Good evening, dear Sir, Mr. Adams.

SENGBE: Eh . . . we are just passing. We are going to Farmington to do concert. Our teacher and the others are waiting. Kale want to give this letter, which he write to Mr. Adams. That is why we stop here.

Hands over the letter.

ADAMS: *(Surprised.)* Kale wrote a letter, himself?

SIMEON: Many of the Africans can, now, read and write, Sir. This has been part of the committee's effort to provide for their physical well-being and their intellectual and religious instruction.

SENGBE: Yes, Sir, Mr. Adams. We are glad we are learning America language. We learn to read and write. We like it very much. Mr. James Covey, he teach us to sing Christian songs in Mende language.

ADAMS: Is that right, little Kale?

KALE: Yes, Sir, Mr. Adams. We talk America language a little. Not very good. We write every day. We write plenty letters. We read most all time. We read Matthew, and Mark, and Luke, and John, and plenty of little books. We love books very much.

SIMEON: Kale, would you like to say grace for Mr. Adams to hear?

KALE: Yes, Sir. Me and Sengbe can sing a Christian song in Mende before I say the grace.

Impressed, the men welcome Kale's idea. Kale and Sengbe sing a Mende version of this song for them:

> Stand up stand up for Jesus
> Ye soldiers of the cross
> Lift high his royal banner
> It must not suffer loss
> From victory on to victory
> His army he shall lead
> Till every foe is vanquished
> And Christ is Lord indeed

Cheers and joy at their achievement.

ADAMS: Well, let's not waste your time any further. We all can just listen to Kale's letter.

SENGBE: Why not read letter yourself?

KALE: Yes. Let me read. Dear friend, Mr. Adams. I want to write a letter to you because you love Mende people and you talk to grand court. We want to tell you one thing. Jose Ruiz say we born in Havana. He tell lie. We all born in Mende country. We want you to ask court what we have done wrong. What for, America people keep us in prison? Some people say, Mende people crazy. Mende people dolt, because we don't talk America language. America people don't talk Mende language. America people dolt? Dear Mr. Adams, you have children. You have friends. You love them. You feel sorry if Mende people come and carry them all to Africa. We feel bad for our friends and friends feel bad for us. If America people give us free, we glad; if they no give us free, we sorry. We sorry for Mende people little. We sorry for America people great deal, because God punish liars. We want you to tell grand court that Mende people don't want to go back to Havana. We no want to be killed. Dear friend, we want you to know how we feel. Mende people think, think, think; nobody know what we think. The teacher, he know how we feel. We tell him some Mende people have got souls. All we want is make us free.

Complete silence follows this most touching reading. Adams breaks the silence.

ADAMS: (*Prayerfully, in accepting the case.*) The world, the flesh, and all the devils in hell are arrayed against any man who now, in the North American union, shall dare to join the standard of the almighty God to put down the African slave trade. And what can I, upon the verge of my seventy-fourth birthday, with a shaken hand, a darkening eye, a drowsy brain, and my faculties dropping from me one by one as the teeth are dropping from my head—what can I do for the cause of God and man for the progress of human emancipation—for the suppression of the African slave trade? Yet, my conscience presses me on—let me but die upon the breach.

Happiness flows in the room at Adams's acceptance. The Amistads embrace Adams.

TAPPAN: We thank you very much, Sir.

SIMEON: May God continue to bless you, Sir.

LEAVITT: Thank you, Sir. This is going to be a historic moment.

ADAMS: Indeed. I am about to take part in an epic battle with the court—clearly on the side of pro-slavery interest. Yet, an inflammation of my left eye threatens me with complete disability to perform my final duty before the Supreme Court, while pressure of preparation threatens that disability. I shall walk to the capital with a thoroughly bewildered mind—this I know—a mind so bewildered as to leave me only with a prayer that presence of mind may not utterly fail me at the time of the trial I am about to go through. Yet, here I go to face the Supreme Court.

Blackout. The song, "Stand up, stand up" rises in the background and fades as lights come on the Supreme Court.

SCENE NINE

A small and packed courtroom. An arched-shaped room, damp, insufficient windows and light. When the lights come on, the court is already in session. The Attorney General *has begun his case, pacing backwards and forwards. Ruiz is already on the witness stand.*

ATT. GEN.: (*Walking back and forth.*) My clients bought forty-nine slaves in Havana and shipped aboard the schooner *La Amistad*. I will now call on my client, Don Jose Ruiz to testify. Now, Don Jose Ruiz, please tell the court what happened on the night in question.

RUIZ: I bought forty-nine slaves in Havana and shipped them onboard the schooner, *La Amistad*. For the first three nights, everything went nice, nice, nice. On the fourth night, I heard a noise in the forecastle. I don't know how things began. It was dark and there was no moon.

ATT. GEN.: Where were you at that time?

RUIZ: All of us were asleep. We were awakened by the noise. (*Pointing at Sengbe.*) Jose! Jose, led the Africans to attack us—the whites! He led the others on deck, where they attacked and killed Capitan Ferrer and Celestino, the cook.

ATT. GEN.: What did you do?

RUIZ: I picked up an oar and tried to quell the mutiny. I cried, "No! No!" Then I heard one of the crew cry, "Murder!" We tried to put up resistance, me and Pedro, but we were greatly outnumbered and had no chance.

ATT. GEN.: Did the blacks attack you directly?

Amistad Kata-Kata

RUIZ: Oh, yes. I was well battered. Jose struck me heavily with a cutlass. I could have been killed also. I could not recall the name of the slave who saved my life. After, he persuaded Jose not to kill me. Jose put his sword to my throat and cried, "Africa! Africa! Land of rising sun! Sail to Africa!" I could have been killed also.

BALDWIN: (*Jumping from his seat.*) Why was your life spared, Senor Ruiz?

RUIZ: According to Jose, they spared our lives, me and Pedro, so that we would sail them back to Africa.

BALDWIN: Senor Don Jose Ruiz, I am putting it to you that your activities were are all illegal and that you tricked the Africans when they ordered you to return them to Africa.

ATT. GEN.: (*Jumping up in objection.*) My Lord, I don't think . . .

JUDGE: Objection overruled. Let the witness answer the question.

RUIZ: Nothing was illegal about our activity. We had purchased the blacks in a public slave market in Havana.

BALDWIN: Jose Ruiz, do you not know that the Spanish law of 1817, which governed Cuba, forbids the importation of blacks from Africa?

RUIZ: I bought all my blacks from the public slave mart in Havana. I never went to Africa.

BALDWIN: And you want to tell the court that you were unaware that the blacks entered Cuba in violation of this law?

RUIZ: I am not aware. (Baldwin *takes his seat.*)

ATT. GEN.: Thank you, your honor. Your honor, I will now invite young Antonio, the cabin boy and slave of Captain Ferrer, who was slain by no less a person than Joseph Cinqué, to take the witness stand. (Antonio *comes forward, takes the oath and the witness stand.*)

ATT. GEN.: What is your name?

ANTONIO: Antonio.

ATT. GEN.: Antonio what?

ANTONIO: Antonio.

ATT. GEN.: What were you doing on board the *Amistad* vessel on that night in question?

ANTONIO: I am a slave and cabin boy of Capitan Ferrer.

ATT. GEN.: (*Pointing to* Sengbe.) Do you know this man?

ANTONIO: Yes.

ATT. GEN.: Where did you first see him?

ANTONIO: In Havana. Six days after our vessel arrived in Havana, Cinqué and the other blacks, including four children, boarded our ship at night.

ATT. GEN.: What happened when the revolt broke out?

ANTONIO: Cinqué killed the Capitan by a machete blow to the forehead. The cook, Celestino, had died earlier. The slaves threw the body of Capitan Ferrer overboard, after Cinqué stole his watch.

ATT. GEN.: Was your life, at any time, threatened?

ANTONIO: Yes. When Cinqué threatened the lives of Pepe, Pedro and me. Lopez (*pointing to one of the slaves*) stopped him. Cinqué tied me by the ankle but Lopez turned me loose. When Cinqué threatened to kill me, Lopez cried, "No! No! Kill boy no good."

BALDWIN: (*Again, jumping up.*) Antonio, it was not Cinqué who killed the Captain.

ANTONIO: Yes. Cinqué did not kill anyone.

BALDWIN: Well then, who killed Captain Ferrer?

ANTONIO: I don't know.

BALDWIN: Your honor, you heard him.

Antonio takes his seat.

ATT. GEN.: My next witness is Lt. Richard W. Meade.

Meade steps on, takes his oath and stands.

ATT. GEN.: What is your name, Sir?

MEADE: Richard W. Meade.

ATT. GEN.: Occupation?

MEADE: An officer in the U.S. Navy.

ATT. GEN.: What is your rank, Sir?

MEADE: Lieutenant.

ATT. GEN.: Good. Lieutenant, what circumstances led to the arrest of the *Amistad* schooner and its cargo. Do you mind telling the court, Sir?

MEADE: I was on duty onboard the American Revenue Cutter, the U.S.S. *Washington*, when I spotted a black schooner with sails torn and tattered, lying low in the water, off Culloden Point. That's less than a mile off Long Island. As I peered through my glass, I saw what appeared to be a dozen men rushing back and forth across the sand, carrying trunks from the small boat, towards some wagons up the shore. As I finally brought the shoreline into focus, I could see that about six of these men were black. The rest were white. Immediately I began to wonder what kind of oppression would involve blacks and whites together.

ATT. GEN.: And what did you do as a responsible officer, Sir?

MEADE: I alerted the commander of the *Washington*, Lieutenant Thomas R. Gedney. After observing the activity and immediately suspecting smuggling, he ordered the mid-shipman, D.D. Porter, to take a boat of six armed men to investigate both the schooner and the people ashore. I volunteered to go with them.

ATT. GEN.: What happened when you reached the ship?

MEADE: We were shocked by the eerie sight. The sides of the once colorful vessel—off-white, separating a black top and a green bottom—were weatherbeaten and covered with barnacles, with seaweed stringing from the cable along the waterline. The topsail was gone. The sails were shredded as they waved lifelessly with the wind. The deck was strewn with stale remains of food, ripped-open boxes, empty medicine containers, torn and tattered silk, cotton, and other materials.

ATT. GEN.: What about the occupants of the vessel?

MEADE: That was the worst sight of all. Perhaps fifty of them, all blacks—one armed with a pistol and cutlass; some had long-bladed knives. Many were half-clothed or even naked. All clearly desperate from hunger and thirst. Four of the blacks were children—three of them girls—standing around the wind glass, and the boy, all probably under thirteen years old. We immediately stripped the blacks of their weapons with absolutely no resistance and took control amidst great excitement and confusion.

ATT. GEN.: When did you first encounter Don Jose Ruiz?

MEADE: Well, at this point, some of my men, who were searching the ship, appeared from the hold accompanied by two haggard white men, severely scarred on their heads and arms from recent injuries. One of them was (*pointing*) him. Ruiz.

ATT. GEN.: Can you tell the court what went on between you and the two battered whites, Sir?

MEADE: I immediately demanded the ship's papers and got them.

ATT. GEN.: What did the papers say?

MEADE: That the ship was a slaver, built in Baltimore, in the U.S.A. I read its name, *La Amistad* and I knew it meant friendship in Spanish.

BALDWIN: (*Jumping up.*) Lt. Meade, did you not suspect that the vessel contained something of value and try to lure all the blacks ashore so that you could seize the vessel as a prize?

MEADE: No, Sir.

BALDWIN: You very well knew that New York, where the ship was captured, had abolished slavery. That was why you took the slave ship and its contents to New London, Connecticut, where slavery was still legal.

MEADE: Yes. I was only doing my duty. According to my inquiry and the papers onboard, the *Amistad* was a Spanish slaver, legally authorized to transport fifty-three ladinos as slaves—belonging to Don Jose Ruiz and Pedro Montez—from Havana to Puerto Principe. The slaves had mutinied and had murdered their Captain and so

Amistad Kata-Kata

apparently guilty of piracy and murder. It is now left with the court to make a ruling.

BALDWIN: From your own judgment, do you think these blacks were ladinos, born in Cuba, or were they just imported from Africa?

MEADE: By their strong African accent, it would well be that they were transported from Africa not very long ago.

BALDWIN: Thank you very much. I have no further questions. (*Gesturing to the Attorney General.*) Mr. Attorney General?

ATT. GEN.: Thank you. It is all clear, my lords. There are documented evidences, right in front of you, signed by the legal authorities concerned. My lords, I have repeated the arguments given in Hartford and New Haven, and the stance outlined to Van Buren in autumn, 1839, by former Attorney General Felix Grundy. Two points of consideration in this case, according to the treaty of 1785, are as follows: 'Due and sufficient proof concerning the property thereof' and, if so, whether the United States had the right to intervene in securing the property of the Spanish claimants. The committee among nations demands that the United States accept ship's papers as 'prima facie' evidence. The issue of the *Amistad* case is not a matter of right and wrong, but whether the granting of the papers fell within the official's authority. The attorneys representing the Africans have failed to prove fraud concerning the Captain General's certificate. The treaties of 1817 and 1835 relate only to the slave trade. They have no bearing on whether the Africans were slaves. The captives are therefore returnable to Spain as property. When American vessels wreck in Cuba, they seek restoration. When an American ship ends up in British possession with slaves aboard, the government in Washington calls for their restoration. The treaty of Ghent in 1814 provided a commission to deal with claims resulting from slaves carried off during the war. The *Antelope* decision upheld the restoration of a captured foreign slaver. A foreign vessel captured in time of peace, engaged in the slave trade, will be restored, even if the nation to which the vessel belonged had prohibited it. It is utterly unfounded and entirely gratuitous to argue the questions about the slave trade and whether my clients knew that the slaves were from Africa. The court's only responsibility is to decide whether the treaty of 1795 required restoration of the blacks to their owners, or whether the American law of 1819 called for their return to Africa.

He takes his seat.

JUDGE: Defense?

BALDWIN: Your honors, I am inviting one of the Africans to take the witness stand. (Fulleh *steps forward and takes the oath.*) What is your name?

FULLEH: My name is Fulleh.

BALDWIN: Where were you born?

FULLEH: I was born in a Mende country in Africa—Sierra Leone.

BALDWIN: Now Fulleh, I want you to tell the court what happened to you.

FULLEH: My own king sell me in Sa Lone to Senor who bring me to Havana and sell me to Senor; who sell me to Ruiz; who bring me here. We all born in Mende country—Sa Lone. (*Pointing at each, in turn.*) Eh . . . Sengbe, Sa Lone; Gabro, Sa Lone; eh . . . Kimbo, Sa, Bona, Kinna, Bongay, Fulwa, Kagne, Kale, we all born in Mende, Sa Lone.

BALDWIN: What happened, Fulleh, after the Senor sold you to Ruiz?

FULLEH: Eh, we forced into vessel. Onboard we have small eat, small drink. And for stealing water which was refused me, I was held down by sailors and Ruiz told them to beat me. I was beaten badly. There was wounds all over my body.

BALDWIN: And then, what happened?

FULLEH: Ruiz tell the sailors to put some mixture on my wounds. It was painful. I wept like a child and my companions wept with me.

BALDWIN: Do you know what kind of mixture?

FULLEH: Yes. They mixed rum and gunpowder and salt.

BALDWIN: Are you sure?

FULLEH: Yes. I am very sure. See. (*Removing his shirt.*) See. The marks are still visible.

Amistad Kata-Kata

BALDWIN: Thank you, Fulleh. Please take your seat. (*Pause, as* Fulleh *steps down.*) Your honors, the evidences are as clear as pure drinking water in a clean tumbler. Apart from being enslaved, the Africans had been whipped and maltreated throughout, and at one point made to believe that they would be killed and prepared for supper upon their arrival. Let me now call on Joseph Cinqué for final examination by the defense. Joseph Cinqué, please take the witness stand. (Sengbe *does not budge.* Baldwin *calls out again.*) Joseph Cinqué, please take the stand.

SENGBE: (*Stands, takes a hard look at* Baldwin.) If it is me you are referring to, please Mr. Baldwin, my name is Sengbe Pieh. Do not call me by another name.

BALDWIN: Sengbe Pieh, is it true that you led a revolt onboard the ship, the *Amistad,* in which you were being transported to slavery?

SENGBE: (*Emphatically.*) Yes.

Silence falls, then weak murmurs before Baldwin *continues.*

BALDWIN: Now Sengbe, please tell the court why you revolted?

SENGBE: I was not born to be a slave. So, it is better for me to die fighting than to live many moons in misery. And if I am hanged, I will be happy if by dying, I will save my black race from bondage. I led my companions to kill Captain Ferrer and Celestino, the cook.

ATT. GEN.: (*Springs up.*) Your honor, this is tantamount to . . .

JUDGE: Overruled.

Attorney General *sits.*

BALDWIN: Sengbe, please tell the court what happened after you had killed the captain and the cook and had taken over.

SENGBE: I spared his life—him and Senor Montez, so that they could sail us back to Africa. But three moons passed, and we were still at sea.

BALDWIN: Why?

SENGBE: They tricked us.

BALDWIN: How? Can you explain?

SENGBE: In the day time, they sailed the ship toward the rising sun—toward Africa. At night, they took advantage and turned the ship to Cuba. We followed a zigzag course for two months. Food and water ran out. I held the command the whole time, forcing the others to conserve food and water. I gave a full ration only to the children and took the smallest portion for myself. Eight of my companions died of hunger, thirst, and cold.

ADAMS: Thank you. Please take your seat. (*Clears his throat.*) Your honors, had he lived in the days of Greece and Rome, his name would have been handed down to posterity as one who has practiced the most sublime of all virtues—disinterested patriotism and un-shrinking courage. Had a white man done it, they would have immortalized him. His name would have been made glorious. Your honors, I have endeavored to show that the Africans, in this case, are entitled to their liberty from this court. Africans were born free and are entitled to their freedom. Those carrying the case against the Africans, including the United States government, maintained that these Africans are slaves and have produced licenses to substantiate this. But, these licenses are patently fraudulent. The laws of Spain forbid slave trade. They were not slaves when captured on Long Island and could not be made slaves thereafter. They knew nothing of the Constitution, law, or language of the country upon which they were, thus, thrown and accused as pirates and murderers, and claimed as slaves by the very men who were then, their captives. They were denied, even, of speech in their own defense. These conditions are calamitous. It demands, from a humane civilized nation as ours, compassion. It demands, from the brotherly love of a Christian land, sympathy. It demands, from a republic professing reverence for the rights of man, justice. But, what are we seeing? What are we experiencing? What have we found? Is this compassion? Is this sympathy? Is this justice? Your honors, my argument on behalf of the defense is closed.

Adams *retires. Silence follows as judges prepare to give their ruling.*

Amistad Kata-Kata

JUDGE: The issue before this court is a very sensitive and delicate one. The Spanish government on behalf of Don Jose Ruiz and Pedro Montez claims that these Africans are the property of those two, said gentlemen, while the Amistad Committee defending the Africans denies that Sengbe Pieh, alias Joseph Cinqué, and the thirty-eight other Negroes are slaves. The evidence in this court is cogent and irresistible that the blacks are natives of Africa, kidnapped in Africa, unlawfully transported to Cuba, and resold in Havana, in violation of the laws of the Kingdom of Spain, which governs Cuba. The U.S. District Attorney has himself admitted in this court of law that the blacks are natives of Africa, recently smuggled from Africa and taken to Cuba. Spanish law in 1820 had abolished the African slave trade and made any participation in it a very heinous crime. When the schooner, *La Amistad*, entered American waters, the blacks were in possession of themselves, claiming their fundamental rights to freedom. (*Pause.*) Sengbe Pieh, alias Joseph Cinqué, and his companions will not sigh for Africa in vain. Bloody as may be their hands, they may yet embrace their kindred. I will put in the form of a decree to this court that these Africans, excepting Antonio, be handed to the President of the United States of America, Martin Van Buren, to be transported to Africa, there to be delivered to the agent appointed to receive and conduct them home. The battle for the Africans' freedom seems to have been won. The captives are free. I have spoken.

There are mixed reactions as court rises for the Judge to leave. As the Amistads bust out with emotions of joy and tears, the prosecution, his face down, shame-facedly sneaks out of the courtroom. Adams goes over and shakes hands with Sengbe before anyone else.

ADAMS: (*To* Sengbe.) Mr. Sengbe Pieh, the end of your ordeal has come. The big court has come to a decision that you—one and all—are free. You are no longer captives. You are free to return home to Sierra Leone, if you so wish. Congratulations, Mr. Sengbe Pieh. Well done. May God, the Almighty, grant you safe passage back home.

SENGBE: (*Emotionally.*) Me, I am glad. Me thank the American man. Me thank you, Mr. Adams. You are the only man in the world who can talk to

America grand court and the grand court listen and answer correct. Me glad. All my people will be glad.

ADAMS: (*To the* Amistad Committee.) Gentlemen, the Africans have won. The Africans are free. We have all won. Thanks in the name of humanity and justice to you.

TAPPAN: Thank you very much, Mr. Adams. We hear you. Thanks in the name of humanity and justice to you, Sir.

SIMEON: Praise the lord, Mr. Adams. May the Lord be with you. Let us thank the Lord and Savior for deliverance from the wicked men in Havana.

ADAMS: Gentlemen, let's give thanks and praise to Mr. Baldwin. I hope you realize what you have done for humanity, Mr. Baldwin.

BALDWIN: Thank you, Sir. You have been a great inspiration for me, Sir. And this applies to all you gentlemen, and, indeed, the Amistad captives. I am glad to be able to serve humanity in this precious way. Though the battle was bitter, the victory is sweet. Thank you. I must leave now.

SENGBE: Let's go and break the news to the others. They are waiting anxiously. (*As they exit,* Kale *stays behind, deep in thought.* Sengbe *returns to find* Kale *alone.*) What is the matter, Kale? Why do you stay behind, alone? Let's go, man. Are you not happy? What are you thinking?

KALE: Sengbe, until we get back to Africa, we are not free.

SENGBE: I know, Kale. I know that very well . . .

KALE: They tell us many times before that we are free and many times they put us in jail again, saying we are not free.

SENGBE: Kale, this is the last. This is final. When our friend, Mr. Adams, say we are free, we are free. He is the big chief of them all in the grand court. Don't you see it on the papers?

KALE: Sengbe, paper lie sometimes.

SENGBE: Come on, Kale. Let's go. Let's not keep the others waiting.

As he pulls Kale by the hand, they break into a song and dance.[5] *Blackout.*

Returning from the ceremony, Grandma *and* Student *dash in.*

GRANDMA: *(Furious.)* No! No! No! I will not take that. What kind of nonsense is this? Why should he refuse to provide a ship to bring them home? Is he not the president? The big chief—in America? Have the grand courts not . . .

STUDENT: Calm down, Grandma. Calm down. Listen . . .

GRANDMA: Don't tell me to calm down. Why should I? Have not the grand courts given the final verdict? Did the judge not rule that my people are free?

STUDENT: Grandma, listen please.

GRANDMA: I will not listen. Enough is enough. If the court say they should be handed over to the President, who must see that they return home, then the President must provide a ship for them. I'm sick and tired of this man.

STUDENT: Grandma, let me explain. Even though President Van Buren refused to provide a ship to bring them home . . .

GRANDMA: But he should. That's his responsibility.

STUDENT: Yes Grandma, but the Amistad Committee took up the responsibility.

GRANDMA: To provide the ship?

STUDENT: Yes, Grandma.

GRANDMA: Hmnn.

STUDENT: Yes, Grandma. They chartered the ship that finally brought them home. The ship was called the *Gentlemen*. Some white men are bad. We have seen. But some are good. We have also seen.

GRANDMA: You are right, my son. Some black men are also bad, whilst others are very, very good. That is how it has been. That is how it is. And that is how it will ever remain.

Blackout.

Hartford. At the departure of the Gentleman *the* Amistads, *the Amistad Committee, and many others are gathered to bid farewell, as* Simeon *leads a prayer.*

SIMEON: (*In prayer.*) I will lift up mine eyes unto the hills, from whence cometh my help.

CHORUS: My help cometh from the Lord, who made Heaven and Earth.

SIMEON: Lift up your hearts.

CHORUS: We lift them up unto the Lord.

SIMEON: As you take leave of us today, I want you, Sengbe, and all of you to know that Christ has watched over you.

CHORUS: Amen.

SIMEON: Christ has raised up friends like us for you.

CHORUS: Amen.

SIMEON: And it is Christ who has influenced the grand court to set you free.

CHORUS: We glad. We love God. We love Jesus Christ He over all. We thank him.

The *Amistad* Revolt

Adapted from the novel *Echo of Lions,*
by Barbara Chase-Riboud

BY YULISA AMADU MADDY

Characters

Celestino
Ramon Ferrer
Antonio
Sengbe Pieh
Slaves / Amistaders
    Kabba Sei
    Kabba Kpekelay
    Sessi
    Fabanna
    Grabeau
    Fulwi
    Burnah
    Fooni
    Bartu
    Shule
    Bau
    Kimbo
    First Born
    Teme
    Kagne
    Magru
    Kale
    Fuliwa
Jacinto
Manuel
Don Jose Ruiz
Don Montez
Chorus
Captain Fordham
Captain Green
MacIntosh (White Farmer)
Colonel Pendleton / Marshall
Mrs. Pendleton
Reverend Gibbs
Vivian Braithwaite
Judge Judson
Lewis Tappan
Baldwin
Staples
Braithwaite
Masked Figures
Girls
Elderly Woman
Bayah Bia
Tau
Maada
First Krooman
Second Krooman
Third Krooman
White Overseer
MaLady
Misi
Sailors
Dockworkers
James Covey
Prosecution-Holabird
Salesman
Martin Van Buren
Forsyth
John Quincy Adams
Louisa Adams
Charles Quincy Adams
Henry D. Gilpin
Egugu Mask

MOVEMENT I

THE REVOLT (ON DECK.)

The stage is in darkness. Dim light reveals projection on screen of a ship flying the Spanish flag. The name "La Amistad" boldly printed on the side of the ship. A towering main mast. Sounds of heavy seas in motion, roaring waves, strong winds and the ship's creaking noises. Overcast gray clouds. Slides with grotesque images of African slaves being captured, loaded onto ships, flogged and tortured. From offstage shouts and sounds of cursing and whipping against crying, wailing, and groans.
    The images go on flashing. Blackout. Light. Celestino, *the Spanish cook, standing on deck watching.* Captain Ferrer *is sitting on a chair sleeping. Some distance away* Antonio *is sitting, dozing. From upstage left* Sengbe Pieh *quietly enters on tiptoe, followed by the* Slaves *brandishing cane knives and cutlasses.*

SENGBE: (*Rushes on* Celestino, *with pent-up venom.*) You die! (*Before* Celestino *can move,* Sengbe *kills him with a stroke of his cutlass.*)

FERRER: (*With sword in hand, followed by* Antonio, *shouting.*) Give them bread. (*Ordering.*) Put down those cutlasses. (Kabba Sei *raises his cutlass, but* Ferrer *runs him through with his sword.*)

SENGBE: (*Shouting.*) Kill the whiteman. Kill! (*Striking* Ferrer *on the head and killing him.*)

Jacinto *and* Manuel *enter from upstage right. The* Slaves *turn on them. They flee shouting "Murder, Mutiny." Chased by* Sengbe, *they go off upstage center.* Don Jose Ruiz *enters downstage right brandishing an oar. He looks round fearfully, drops the oar and runs back chased by* Kabba Kpekelay *and* Sessi. Don Montez, *coming from downstage right armed with a club and a knife, comes face-to-face with* Fabanna, *matchet raised.* Don Montez *half-parries and gets gashed on the head. Another blow from* Fabanna's *matchet rips open his arm.* Montez *drops his weapons and flees, chased by* Fabanna *and* Grabeau. Sengbe *returns. He looks around, angry and desperate.*

65

SENGBE: (*To the others.*) They jumped into the sea.

FULWI: (*Laughing.*) They will catch land at the bottom of the sea with the water daemons.

Ruiz *and* Antonio *are dragged onto the stage by* Kabba Kpekelay *and* Sessi. *At the same time* Fabanna *and* Grabeau *push the wounded* Montez *onto the stage.* Sengbe *raises his cutlass walking slowly toward* Montez.

BURNAH: (*Moves between* Sengbe *and* Montez.) No! He can sail us back to Mendeland.

FOONI: (*Pointing to* Antonio.) And he will interpret for us.

SENGBE: (*To* Montez.) You will take us back to Africa.

MONTEZ: (*Collapses onto the floor.*) I don't know how. I can't do it. I can't. I can't.

RUIZ: (*Between his teeth.*) If you don't we are DEAD! Dead!

SENGBE: (*Ordering.*) Chain them. (Grabeau, Fooni, *and* Bartu *put them to sit.*) You whitemen say iron chains are good for Mendemen. They are good for whitemen. Yes? (Shule *and* Bau *go off to get the chains.*) You whitemen say one cup of water a day is enough for Mendemen, then one cup of water a day is enough for whitemen.

KIMBO: (*Pointing to the bodies of* Ferrer *and* Celestino.) What do we do with them? (Shule *and* Bau *return with the chains.*)

SENGBE: We send them to the water demons at the bottom of the sea. (Fabanna *orders* Montez, Ruiz, *and* Antonio *to take the bodies offstage.*)

SESSI: And Kabba Sei and First Born?

SENGBE: We pray to Gewoh that their spirits will return home and rest peacefully in Mendeland with the ancestors.

The bodies of First Born *and* Kabba Sei *are placed center stage.* Montez, Antonio, Ruiz *and* Fabanna *return.* Montez, Antonio, *and* Ruiz *are made to sit upstage left and chained.* Sengbe *leads the chant and performs the Mende traditional death ritual. The four children, three girls,* Teme, Kagne, Margru, *and the boy,* Kale, *are put in the care of* Fuliwa.

The *Amistad* Revolt

SOLO:	Ah mii Gewoh la to
CHORUS:	Gewoh la to
SOLO:	Gewoh la to
CHORUS:	Gewoh la to
	Gewoh la to
	Gewoh la to
	Khuna foh
SOLO:	Ge lingi ayaa
CHORUS:	Ge lingi ayaa
SOLO:	Ge lingi ayaa
CHORUS:	Ge lingi aya
	Ge lingi aya
	Ge lingi aya
	Khuna foh
SOLO:	Ge me yeh vehn
CHORUS:	Ge me yeh vehn
SOLO:	Ge me yeh vehn
CHORUS:	Ge me yeh vehn
	Ge me yeh vehn
	Ge me yeh vehn
	Khuna foh.

After the two bodies have been lowered to the sea, Sengbe *and the men search the ship, bringing out clothes, drinks, and food. They go on to dress themselves. The spectacle is at once interesting and ridiculous. They drink, dance, sing, and make merry as well as mocking the two* Spaniards *and the half-caste,* Antonio.

SENGBE: You now. (*Signaling them to get up and move toward the audience. They struggle up and stumble as they move.*) You name! Name! Name! (*He goes on prodding them.*)

ANTONIO: Antonio Ferrer. (*The Amistad Africans laugh, mocking him.*)

KIMBO: (*Sings.*) Antonio Ferrer
Antonio Ferrer
You are not Antonio Ferrer
You mama was raped by the masa.

ANTONIO: I don't know my mama
I don't know my papa
I don't know no other name
My massa call me Antonio Ferrer.

Sengbe rips Antonio's shirts off, pushes him down, turning his back to the audience, revealing where he was branded on the back with an 'S' (slave). Sengbe starts to chant and the others join, except the three.

Blackout. Thunder rolls followed by lightning. Sound of heavy rains falling. Several heavy gun shots.

SENGBE: (*Shouting in the dark, hysterical.*) Take them below and lock them . . . Go now!

Blackout.

SAG HARBOR

Slides flashing on screen—SAG HARBOR. Distant landscape. Blue mists, trees and houses. Flashes of La Amistad's *sails in shreds, paint peeling, deck filthy. Tired, hungry, and desperate faces. Bodies sprawl lifelessly on the deck. Light up on the shore.*

CAPTAIN FORDHAM: (*Excited.*) I swear to God, Henry, we've caught up with that damned pirate ship the newspapers have all been ravin' 'bout.

CAPTAIN GREEN: And with the pirates as well. (*Looking offstage though spyglass.*) Here, take a look . . .

FORDHAM: (*Looking through spyglass.*) Sweet Jesus, Mary of the Immaculate Conception.

CAPTAIN GREEN: Can you make out the name of the schooner?

The *Amistad* Revolt

FORDHAM: Looks to me like the ALMEDA.

GREEN: What kind of name is that for a ship?

Sengbe enters followed by Antonio, Fooni, Burnah, Grabeau, Bartu, and Sessi. Sengbe wears a planter's jacket and hat. Others have loincloths and shawls.

FORDHAM: Look! What the hell kind of sailors are those coming toward us?

The two captains race to meet Sengbe and his men.

GREEN: More than two weeks ago the *Emmeline* tried to take that pirate schooner in tow, but those pirates were armed with sugar cane knives and cutlasses, and they cast her off.

FORDHAM: Bush savages in flesh for real.

Sengbe gestures greeting to the two men. A white Farmer comes running to join them.

SENGBE: Africa! (*Grabeau mimes swimming and calls out: Africa.*)

FORDHAM: Swim to Africa.

Sengbe holds out a handful of gold doubloons.

GREEN: I think they want us to sail their asses to Africa.

Sengbe brings out some more coins.

FORDHAM: (*Greedily.*) Not a bad idea. They certainly have enough gold on that ship to pay somebody to sail them home.

GREEN: And they have a ship. A seaworthy ship.

FORDHAM: How many days?

GREEN: Thirty to forty, sailing with the wind.

FORDHAM: How does one get back from Africa?

GREEN: The ship. The ship is worth a fortune.

FORDHAM: And we can even pick up a few hundred slaves coming back.

GREEN: (*To* Sengbe.) Where? Where in Africa?

FORDHAM: Most slaves come from the Windward coast.

GREEN: Now, where? Where, you niggers? Where the hell in Africa?

FORDHAM: (*Reeling off names.* River Congo, Niger, Gallinas?

SENGBE: (*Joined by others.*) Gallinas, Gallinas.

MACINTOSH: I don sold my two dogs and sacks of potatoes to them. (*He shows the coins.*)

FORDHAM: I thought you loved those dogs.

GREEN: MacIntosh will sell his mother for a Spanish doubloon.

FORDHAM: You know what they do to dogs in Africa? They eat them. They are cannibals. They eat people. Do you know that?

MACINTOSH: Looks like these folks are lost. I means lost. They sure could do with some help.

GREEN: I'll do it.

FORDHAM: First, somebody must warn the Coast Guard or the Navy.

MACINTOSH: We've been spotting that ship. It appears and disappears like a phantom ship with her tattered sails, no flag and no destination.

GREEN: I'll sail you fellers to Gallinas for all the gold you've got on the schooner, minus the rations and supplies for the voyage, plus the ship. Is it a deal? (*Pause. He shouts.*) Galliness, Galliness.

SENGBE: (*Nods approval. The others shout.*) Galliness, Galliness.

VOICE: (*Shouting.*) The *Washington.* The *Washington.* (Sengbe *runs offstage. He is immediately brought back in handcuffs by three white sailors carrying a gun, followed by* Lieutenant Gedney.)

GEDNEY: (*Using a loud hailer.*) In the name of the United States, you are under arrest . . .

MACINTOSH: Don't shoot him. He has gold and lots of it.

The *Amistad* Revolt

SENGBE: (*Strongly resisting and shouting to his men. A few of them are walking a distance behind him.*) So make the whitemen kill you by killing them . . . No fear! No fear!

GEDNEY: You are under arrest. I command you to surrender without resistance.

SENGBE: (*Quietly.*) Save yourselves from the whiteman. I know they will hang me.

Blackout.

FIRST VOICE (PENDLETON): The United States District Court Judge for Connecticut, Andrew T. Judson, had to make an immediate decision. A crime had been committed, but by whom? And what punishment, if any, should be meted out, and under whose jurisdiction? Judge Judson is President Van Buren's man and a known enemy of the Negro. He wanted these Black insurrectionists and murderers out of his district. This was an unprecedented legal case.

MRS. PENDLETON: Andrew T. Judson, do you know him? Had to make a decision. (*Emphasis.*) An immediate decision on those murdering, savage pirates of the schooner *Amistad*. Crimes had been committed on that schooner, but by whom? Someone, some people have to be punished, but who? And what should be the punishment, and under whose jurisdiction? Judge Judson is a good friend of President Van Buren, whose winning of the presidency come the next election depends upon the pro-slavery southroons. But more than that, Judson wanted those Black insurrectionists and murderers out of his district, wouldn't you? We don't want a Nat Turner here. And we already drove out Prudence Crandall . . . ha-ha-ha . . . that was something else.

Prudence Crandall teaching:
    nigger girls to read
    nigger girls to count
    nigger girls reading geography
Prudence Crandall was wiped out by Judson.
Prudence Crandall is gone. Married to Mr. . . . I don't even know his name, do you? Oh, I don't care to know his name.

JUDICIAL INVESTIGATION

SECOND VOICE (GIBBS): At anchor, on board the U.S. cutter *Washington* commanded by Lieutenant Gedney, New London, August 29th, 1839.

His Honor Andrew T. Judson, U.S. District Judge on the bench, C.A. Ingersoll, esq. appearing for the U.S. District Attorney. The court was opened by the U.S. Marshal.[1]

Antonio, the slave of the murdered Captain Ferrer, was called before the court.

Don Pedro Montez, owner of part of the cargo, Don Jose Ruiz, also owner of part of the cargo, were heard. Lieutenant Richard Meade acted as interpreter between the Spaniards and the court.

VIVIAN: No one appeared on behalf of the Amistad Africans nor was any communication held with them, but after this examination, the adults, numbering thirty-eight, since eleven had died, were committed for trial for murder on the high seas and piracy, to be held at Hartford on the 17th of September.

PENDLETON: Antonio and the four small children were committed as witnesses. The entire lot were then transferred to the jail, in New Haven, Connecticut.

The sound of church bells tolling. Slowly other bells join in, creating a cacophony of bell sounds. Voices singing offstage the "Pilgrim song."

Sengbe and others are seated on the floor downstage left. A U.S. Marshal—Pendleton—is standing guard. Montez and Ruiz are upstage center, talking to Judge Judson. Gibbs, Tappan, Baldwin, Staples, Braithwaite and his daughter, Vivian, are standing away some distance. Antonio is downstage taunting Sengbe and others. The Marshal is indifferent to Antonio's taunts. Rather, he is enjoying every bit of it.

MONTEZ: (*Walks down to where Sengbe and others are sitting. A broad smile on his face.*) (*To Sengbe*) I own you. You are my property. My slaves. All of you.

ANTONIO: Slaves. (*He laughs. Grabeau trips him, he falls. The Marshal brandishes his fist in front of Grabeau, threatening.*)

The *Amistad* Revolt

Judge Judson *gets up and beckons to the* Marshal *who in turn orders the group to move out.* Judge Judson *exits upstage center.* Sengbe *and others exit upstage right followed by* Antonio *and the* Marshal. Montez *watches them go. He crosses over to* Ruiz *upstage center. They talk in whispers, suspiciously eyeing* Gibbs *and the others. They go off.*

TAPPAN: (*Furious.*) Who owns who?

STAPLES: Outside of the habeas corpus, we have five libels.

VIVIAN: (*Muttering.*) God help them! God! Please, please help free them from the persecution of that cruel Judge Judson.

GIBBS: God will show us the way to help them. Nothing like this ever happened in New Haven before. This is God's divine providence. I mean their arrival. Through them Christianization will get to darkest Africa. They will be given religious instruction.

BRAITHWAITE: No one speaks their language and they don't understand English.

VIVIAN: No one wants to know their story.

GIBBS: If they speak in tongues, why God will make sure his message gets through. The Reverend Leonard Bacon, Henry Ludlow, and Amos Townsend, Jr. will come to their help. (*Shaking his head.*)[2]

BALDWIN: We will fight all the five libels to the end. To the bitter end.

STAPLES: Lieutenant Gedney, the commander of the brig *Washington*, has filed a libel in the district court for the schooner.

BALDWIN: THIS is not going to be a trial about men. It is a trial about GREED.

STAPLES: Captains Green and Fordham, alleging they had captured the Negroes and held them on shore until the *Washington* made its capture, have filed a second libel.

VIVIAN: NOW? Who owns what? Who owns who?

STAPLES: Thirdly, Don Ruiz and Don Montez have filed claims to the Negroes as their slaves and cargo.

BALDWIN: Ours is the task of a defense without precedence. The defense of property versus men, the Law of Nations versus Natural law, northroons versus southroons, slavery versus abolition, rebellion versus liberation.

STAPLES: The fourth libel is ludicrous. Some Cuban merchants, a company who call themselves Tellineas and Aspe put claim to certain merchandise which was on board the *La Amistad*.

BALDWIN: Whatever their claims, these Amistad Africans cannot be held or delivered as property, cargo, or merchandise, for they are not slaves. If the President of the United States persists in his interference, trying to reduce them to the condition of property, it would be a violation of the First Amendment.

STAPLES: Fifth and final libel. The Minister Plenipotentiary of Spain has claimed the slaves and cargo under the treaty between the United States and Spain.

BALDWIN: (*Agitated.*) Our government knows very well that the government of Great Britain paid the government of Spain two million dollars to induce them to give up the slave traffic; and the United States government has agreed to cooperate with Great Britain in putting an end to the damned traffic.

STAPLES: But our government is being called upon, through the person of the President, to become auxiliary to persons engaged in this foul traffic.

After a pause Reverend Gibbs *smiles, shaking hands with* Baldwin *and* Staples.

GIBBS: Gentlemen, Mr. Louis Tappan is on his way from New York. I am going over to the jailhouse and try to get the story from these men. Before we can help them, we have to know their story.

Blackout.

The jailhouse. Sengbe is lying on the floor, a blanket covering his naked body. His mind drifting, dreaming. Tears running down his cheeks. Other prisoners lying sleeping and snoring. Slow fade to misty surroundings. A frondless palm tree center stage. Projection of a mountainous terrain. A few mud huts. Pastoral setting. The resounding blue monotony of a single drum builds from low to high and recedes into the distance. Mask figures enter

The Amistad Revolt

from different directions. They assemble, forming a circle, sitting around the palm tree. Light comes up focusing on a lone tall figure (downstage left) in a long tattered multicolored gown. The mask figures (spirits) sit, heads bowed and still.

SENGBE: Bu-wa
Bu-wa n'gai ma
N'yhanga nunga bu-wa ayaa (*Repeat*)
T'shoo-bo-ayaa
T'shoo-bo-ayaa
T'shoo-bo-ayaa

MASKS: Ayaa!

SENGBE: Bu-wa
Bu-wa n'gai ma
N'yhanga nunga bu-wa ayaa (*Repeat*)

MASKS: 'e yoo oh
'e yoo (oh) n'ga bu-wa
'e yoo n'ga bu-wa
'e yoo.

Gradually the other Amistad Africans enter in the dream. They join hands singing, performing their ritual. The masks go off in the different directions they had come. Lights change to daytime in an African village. Men and Women going about their business as usual. A typical African farming village. People greeting each other. A few Girls coming from the stream. They relax talking and start to play and sing. An Elderly Woman comes and sends them off home.

BAYEH BIA: (*Sengbe's wife—a wrapper around her, she carries a baby on her arm. She is sitting feeding two other children. Another Woman, younger, tall, pregnant, enters with a tray of food which she puts down in front of Bayeh Bia. She sits and they both eat from the same dish and converse. Maada, Sengbe's father, comes by and observes. The two women leave their food to pay him curtsey.*) Papa, sit and let me bring you your food.

TAU: It is my duty. I will bring Papa's food.

BAYEH BIA: I will get him water.

MAADA: Where is Sengbe? He is late returning from the farm.

BAYEH BIA: The harvest will be good, so they work and forget about the time to return home. *(She goes.)*

TAU: *(Coming with tray of food.)* Papa, we cooked your special cassava leaf with beans and okra. *(Bayeh Bia returns with water.)*

MAADA: Sengbe has the most beautiful wives, the best of sisters in our village.

BAYEH BIA: He is our brother, our friend.

TAU: Our lover and a good father.

BAYEH BIA: And so are you, Papa.

MAADA: *(Opening the tray of food.)* I will eat. You feed the children.

Enter Sengbe, both wives go to greet him. He proceeds to greet his father. Tau exits to get water for his bath. Sengbe plays with the children. Bayeh Bia sets about arranging a make-shift dining table. Sengbe exits carrying the children. After a while he re-appears in a wrapper. Goes to sit by his father. He examines his food. Bayeh Bia and Tau sit by him and watch him eat. A long strained flute music in the distance floats in.

SENGBE: The trial is coming in three days. I will leave tonight with Kabba Sei.

BAYEH BIA: I will be glad when it is all over.

MAADA: Go tonight? Why tonight?

SENGBE: The farm. I must be back to oversee the work on the farm. The harvest will be good.

MAADA: *(To Tau)* Let them bring palm wine. My son, I am proud of you. We must pour libation together before you leave.

KABBA SEI: *(Entering in a hurry. Pays his respects.)* Sengbe, we must go. You are not ready?

MAADA: Have you eaten?

KABBA SEI: Yes, Maada.

The *Amistad* Revolt

MAADA: So, you must give him time to eat.

BAYEH BIA: Do you have to travel tonight?

SENGBE: We have to. (*He goes off.*)

KABBA SEI: The others will be there and that viceroy and the chief won't like it if we get there late.

BAYEH BIA: My heart tells me you should not go tonight. (Sengbe *returns.*)

SENGBE: We must go. (*He takes leave of everyone. Exit followed by* Kabba Sei.)

Light fades. Thudding drums rise to a crescendo and stop. Strained flute music plays in the background. Dim light. Sengbe and others on the road carrying spears singing as they go.

SOLO: Atu walli duru ka-ni ayaa

CHORUS: Duru ka-ni

SOLO: Atu walla duru ka-ni

CHORUS: Du ru ka-ni
          Du ru ka-ni
          Wah-na wah dae wah nah-wah
          Wan—ah—wah
          Wan—ah—wah
          tee wara tu-la-hy-dae ayaa
          ai yaee (*fade out*).

Midnight, sudden and sharp, hornblow, long and piercing. The tabulae drum thuds, calling the people.[3] *The people come out from everywhere.* Bayeh Bia, Tau, Maada, *and others.*

FIRST KROOMAN: (*Accompanied by three others. He's tough and in a hurry.*) Message. I have message for you all.

SECOND KROOMAN: (*Blows a whistle.*) Our master want his debt paid tonight.

THIRD KROOMAN: Sengbe Pieh and Kabba Sei have been taken on war road . . . for debt. (Bayeh Bia *and* Tau *throw themselves on the ground crying and shouting.*)

MAADA: (*Surprised.*) Taken on War Road?

> *The three Kroomen produce pistols, shoot into the crowd. Light goes out. Shouts and wails and moans continue in the dark. The women scream. Their screams piercing, trail away into the dark distance. Fade out and in on a now deserted village. Maada weaving a wrapper, sitting on a bench. From a distance, singing can be heard. Maada sings along with the voices offstage.*

VOICES OFFSTAGE: I remember yesterday
    I remember yesterday
    Oh yes! Oh yes! Oh yes!
    I remember yesterday.

    (*Repeat*)

    (*Calls out*) Sengbe Pieh
    I remember yesteryear
    1839 on War Road
    I remember yesteryear
    Mayagilalo stole my son
    Oh yes Oh yes Oh yes
    He gave my son, Sengbe, in exchange for his debt to Vai king
    Manna Siaka
    I remember yesteryear.

    I remember yesteryear
    Sengbe and Kabba Sei went to settle a palaver,
    I remember yesterday day
    Sengbe and Kabba Sei never came back
    Oh yes Oh yes Oh yes
    Soon after, Mayagilalo and his Kroomen
    Invaded my village and took
    Young men, women and children
    I remember yesterday.

    I remember yesteryear
    I remember yesteryear

The *Amistad* Revolt

Oh yes! Oh yes! Oh yes!
I remember yesteryear.

Have you seen Sengbe Pieh for me?
Have you seen Kabba Sei for me?
Oh yes Oh yes Oh yes
I remember yesterday.

Have you seen Bayah Bia for me?
Have you seen Tau for me?
Do please Do please, I beg
Tell me where they are.

MAADA: *(To the audience.)* It is a tradition that I must break kola nuts and pour libation to the ancestors every year. For one hundred and fifty years ago was when it all happened, here in Mani, Mende country. *(He takes a kola from a cloth pouch and breaks a white and red kola nut into four pieces. Takes a cup of water and a bottle of rum which he opens.)* No one can tell your story for you. The story of the Amistad Africans led by Sengbe Pieh is the story that no one can tell except we who know the ancestry of Sengbe Pieh. We are the ones who lost our ancestors to slavery. *(He talks quietly and throws the kola nuts in the air; watches them fall. Excited, he shouts.)* The ancestors have answered. *(He takes a cup of water and bottle of rum. Pours the rum and speaks to himself. He then pours water. Takes a drink from the bottle and then a sip of the water. He replaces them on the ground. Chains clinking, groaning, wailing coming from offstage.)* Listen, I am the eyes and ears of the ancestors. The messenger and medium. I am Maada, the grandfather.

I know what I see
I see what the ancestors want me to see
I need no mortal eyes to look
Into the past to foretell the future
All light:
Daylight, nightlight, yesterlight, and tomorrow's light
I seek, and find.

VOICES: (*Singing.*)

> Sengbe *and others chained.* Men, Women, *and* Children *enter helpless, exhausted, singing. A* White Overseer *brandishes his whip. Some stumble and fall only to be pulled up, kicked and pushed to move on.*

CHORUS: Rolling rolling deep and wide
We are gone away from home
Wind and water scream and cry
We are gone away from home.

SENGBE: How many roads have I crossed in my life
How many battles have I fought
Someone must save us from this murderous clan
Someone must hear our cry.

CHORUS: Rolling rolling deep and wide
We are gone away from home
Wind and water scream and cry
We are gone away from home.

SENGBE: Where is the land which once was mine
Where are my wives and children
Someone must take the blame for this plunder
Someone will have to pay.

CHORUS: Rolling rolling deep and wide
We are gone away from home
Wind and water scream and cry
We are gone away from home.

BAYEH BIA: Why must I wear the chain of iron
Why must I stand naked in shame
Someone must pity my arm where I've bled
Someone must share my pain.

CHORUS: Rolling rolling deep and wide
We are gone away from home
Wind and water scream and cry
We are gone away from home.

The *Amistad* Revolt

TAU: Where is the father of my child
Where is the rock of my life
Someone must hold me and bless my head
Someone must warm my bed.

CHORUS: Rolling rolling deep and wide
We are gone away from home
Wind and water scream and cry
We are gone away from home.

SENGBE: How it is the blood so hot within my veins
The terrible fire of sun on flesh
Oh Gewoh! I screamed and screamed
They whip us, whip us
Their leather snake carved whole roads
Into our flesh.

BURNAH: Pain! Pain can grow stronger than the deepest fear. We see other slaves working in plantation. A contrast. They have been a long time in captivity.

CHORUS: (*Singing.*) Slaver man ah plant your cotton
Slaver man ah cut your cane
Bend mah back in the cruel sunshine
Swing mah arm in the sweepin' rain.

MALADY: Slaver man
Let mah man go
Whiteman
Let him go
May head is achin'
My eyes are red
I need a spirit
That is never dead.

CHORUS: Slaver man ah clean you house
Slaver man ah wash you filth
Bend mah back mornin', noon, and night
You makin' sure you bleed me dead.

MALADY: Slaver man
Ain't you tired?

>   Slaver man
>   What you want?
>   My man is bleedin'
>   He goin' to die
>   I need his spirit
>   Like you need you wife.

SENGBE: Blackness raging inside
Begs me in a thousand screaming pleading
Ways each day to summon murder from my soul.
(*Drums thudding.*)

CHORUS: Call out ancient justice.

BAU: An eye for an eye.

CHORUS: (*Angry.*) Their tongue wild red in their heads
Eyes blue, green, and gray, and wilder
Burning like rude flames
Sweating floods of greed of lust
Wild uncontrolled flames.

MALADY: The wild-eyed slavers
And their whip masters
Rage and rant and rave
Heaping curses, whipping
On horses, round the greeneries
On their land.

MISI: When the leather snake whistles as it falls
To cut sharp and harsh through skin to flesh
To draw blood—red fresh blood
Watch the red torrent rage
Down all those black backs.
The whip snakes through so many times
Whining wild and relentless
Begging for blood, more blood
Pain is deeper than deep love
And the deepest love is fear.

Fade to the jailhouse. Gibbs *is standing by the side of* Sengbe. *He opens his eyes and they stare at each other.*

The *Amistad* Revolt

GIBBS: (*Introducing himself.*) My name is Gibbs, Gibbs, Gibbs. (*The other Prisoners jump up. Sengbe sits and watches and listens without a movement. Gibbs beckons Sengbe to follow him. The Marshal and other prisoners watch as Sengbe reluctantly wraps his blanket and follows. Lights fade out.*)

Downstage. Henry Braithwaite *and daughter* Vivian *strolling back.*

VIVIAN: (*Excited.*) Black men without masters, claiming to be free Africans.

BRAITHWAITE: Speaking a language no one could understand.

VIVIAN: Demanding justice.

BRAITHWAITE: Their leader resisting arrest and inciting his men to attack.

VIVIAN: A foreign African warrior prince. (*A sudden fear.*) Daddy, daddy, we must help them. We must—we must or they will . . . (*She gasps and faints with horror into her father's arms. Upstage center* Prosecution Attorney Judson *appears in silhouette. Addressing the jury—the Prudence Crandall case.* Braithwaite *reminisces.*)

JUDSON: (*To a jury.*) . . . There has ever been in this country a marked difference between the blacks and white men. There is still that difference, and it is impossible to do away with it. Those who claim to be the exclusive philanthropists of the day will tell you this is prejudice. I give it no such name. It is entitled to no such appellation. It is a national pride and national honor which mark this distinction. The white men were oppressed and taxed by the king. They assembled in convention, and at the peril of their lives declared this WHITE NATION free and independent. It was a nation of white men who formed and have administered our government and every American should indulge that PRIDE and HONOR, which is falsely called prejudice, and teach it to his children. Nothing else will preserve the AMERICAN NAME or the AMERICAN CHARACTER. Who of you would like to see the glory of this nation stripped away and given to another race of men? The present is a scheme, cunningly devised, to destroy the rich inheritance left by your fathers. The professed object— as we understand from Prudence Crandall—is to educate the blacks, but the real object is to make people yield their assent by degrees, to this universal amalgamation of the two races. And have the African race be placed on the footing of perfect equality with the AMERICANS. Blacks are not citizens. The Declaration of Independence does not apply to blacks: it concerns only the relations of WHITE colonists with Great Britain and does not speak of their relations with their slaves. Even the Constitution does not claim that Blacks are equals to whites.

The stage in half lights. Pandemonium. Shouting and crying of Black girls. Flashes on screen show an academy building on fire. Flashes continue. The sign "Abolitionist Quaker Academy for Young Ladies" appears on the screen.

FEMALE VOICES: (*Shouting and screaming.*) Fire! Fire! (*Running about terrified in their nightdresses.*)

MALE AND FEMALE VOICES: Kill the nigger girls! Kill the nigger girls!

JUDSON: It is forbidden, under penalty of prison, to establish a school in any town in Connecticut, for colored people not of Connecticut, or teaching, boarding, or harboring Negroes out of state.

BRAITHWAITE: And they marched Prudence Crandall off to jail. (*Pause.*) They locked her up in the cell vacated by a condemned murderer who had been hanged.

VIVIAN: She was only helping Colored girls

Learn to read and write.

VOICES (OFFSTAGE): (*Shouting angrily.*) Kill the nigger girls! Kill the nigger girls!

Blackout.

Cross fade. Flashes on screen. New York Harbor. Dr. Gibbs on stage. A crowd of Sailors, Dockworkers, etc. move about.

GIBBS: Eta . . . fili . . . kiauwa . . . naeni (*counts aloud as he walks about repeating himself*). There must be someone who will understand their language . . . Eta, Fili, kiauwa, naeni. In order to defend themselves and

The *Amistad* Revolt

understand the accusations against them we must get an interpreter. (*Clearing his throat.*) Eta, fili, kiauwa, naeni. (*A handsome young Black man looks around and, laughing loudly, he takes up the counting.*)

COVEY: Loelu, weta, wufura.

GIBBS: (*With excitement, joins with Covey.*) wayapa, tau, pu!

COVEY: My name is Covey, James Covey.

GIBBS: You speak and write the King's English?

COVEY: The Queen's English, sir. But the language you were counting in is Mende and I am Mende. And yes, I do speak and write the Queen's English.

GIBBS: I believe in providence and in miracles. I believe in the conversion of souls. Do you?

COVEY: I am a sailor with the British cruiser *The Buzzard*. Captain Fitzgerald is my adopted father so to speak. About believing in conversion and miracles, well, yes, because I was a slave on the slaver *Henrietta* when we were rescued by the brig of war *Aden*, twelve years ago.

GIBBS: You heard of the Amistad Africans?

COVEY: Yes.

GIBBS: Can you help us defend them by agreeing to be their interpreter?

COVEY: Yes. But I will have to get permission from Captain Fitzgerald.

GIBBS: By all means. By all means.

COVEY: Come with me, sir.

GIBBS: (*As they go.*) Three men have formed the Amistad Defense Committee. We are going to meet them once you obtain permission from Captain Fitzgerald.

Covey: I don't envisage any problem.

GIBBS: Good! These three men I am talking about are millionaires. They are Lewis Tappan, Reverend Joshua Leavitt, and Simeon Jocelyn. The *Amistad* is a Godsend. Until now, all we abolitionists could do was hold meetings and recruit members in the North. Joseph Cinqué has changed all that. He has become the standard of a whole new battle ... (*Cross fade to the jailhouse. Singing in the background.*)

VOICES: (*Humming, then breaking into soft singing.*) And before I be a slave (*song continues*).

SENGBE: (*Behind bars with the others. Crowd files past.* Colonel Pendleton *collects money from them.* Vivian *comes in carrying bread, fruits, sweets which she gives to the children and* Sengbe. Vivian *stands by the cell staring with lingering, infuriating questions she was unable to communicate to* Sengbe. *As* Sengbe *looks back, his voice comes over.*)

> I who was born
> Born like you or you
> Having everything
> I who have a country
> I who have land and lots of land
> I who have a family
> I who have a soul
> All caring, sharing and loving
> I who have feeling
> Have nothing
> Nothing now
> Nothing at all
> You see
> They say
> I am a savage, a beast
> They say I am not human
> I can't think
> I can't see
> I can't feel
> I have no dreams
> No opinion
> No rights of my own
> They say I am a property
> Their property.

(Vivian *turns and walks away, trembling as if she was going to be sick.*)

VIVIAN: (*As she walks away.*) How they peered and leered at them without modesty, without decency, without compassion. Oh God help free them. Help them to go free from these barbarians who profess to be God-fearing Christians.

> Oh God! Oh God!
> Whose liberty have we found
> Whose love must we know
> And the river overcomes the rock
> And mountain
> Running, running clear
> Bright and black and golden in the sun
> Just like a song
> Just like a song.

She exits seeing Gibbs *and* Covey *approach.* Covey *watches her go. In a hurry.* Pendleton *enters, walks past* Gibbs, *who calls out to him.*

GIBBS: We want to see the captives.

PENDLETON: Not until after they've been fed.

GIBBS: We have to talk to them.

PENDLETON: They are hungry.

GIBBS: We won't be long.

PENDLETON: (*Pretending to be thinking.*) OK! But make it short. (*He leads the way and the others follow.*)

Greetings in Mende as they enter. The Captives *leap to their feet and rush to meet him.* Sengbe *comes in. A complete pause as the eyes of the two meet. They hold out their fists and then touch knuckles and finally embrace.*

COVEY: (*Whispering.*) Sangbei.

SENGBE: (*Also whispering.*) Kanela.

GRABEAU: (*Tears in his eyes.*) Take us away.

SENGBE: Tell them what really happened. Tell them we won the war. Ruiz and Montez have lied. Lied to everyone and we have no voice except that of that wretch (*points to* Antonio) and Burnah—once they have our story, they will set us free. (*Pauses and looks around.*) Tell them also of our suffering. Of the ship that brought us across from Lomboko.

BARTU: Is there more beauty here
Is there more beauty in this stone-walled jail
Of the western city
Where is the beauty in the whip
They dragged me across blue miles of water
To meet? Where is the beauty?

CHORUS: And our names now hidden
Even our names hidden.
Who are we?
The leopard and the lion
The antelope and the elephant
Who are we?

Solo drum, fast and furious.

FULIWA: In the throes of the last moon
They stole our prince
They bound our prince in chains
And marched him through hot paths
Wild and bloody, hungry and thirsty
They stole our prince.

Slow drumming, uninterrupted.[4]

GRABEAU: In our village we had wars, we had famine, plagues, but I never dreamed of what one race, one man, could inflict upon another until now.

SESSI: My wife was taken with me. They made me watch as they raped her, one after the other until she . . . she . . . (*He breaks down crying.*)

FULIWA: (*Slowly.*) My brothers! My sisters! My old fathers and mothers. The hardships on the *Teçora*. I better leave it all buried inside . . . yes! I better.

The *Amistad* Revolt

KIMBO: My father was the king's adviser until he died. (*Laughs bitterly.*) After his death the king made our family his slaves. He gave me away as a present to Prince Banga of Bullom who in turn sold me to slavery in Lomboko.

BURNAH: After my father died, I lived with my eldest brother who had many wives. I used to own my own farm and a boat. My brother got very jealous of me. He got me kidnapped and sold into slavery. I know some English and a little about sailing. I used to pass on the order of Sengbe Pieh to the Spanish Montez and Ruiz.

COVEY: Tell me about them: Montez and Ruiz. What kind of whitemen are they?

BURNAH: They do not believe that we are men like they are. They are greedy for slaves and are capable of great and inhuman cruelty. (*Throwing off his blanket.*) I have the scars to prove it. Sengbe is the one who has saved us.

FULIWA: I am a singer. A poet. I am married and have a family. I have a sister I love very much, Sula. I was seized by two men on the way to the river field and they took me to Lomboko and sold me to Luis.

COVEY: Where are the children?

GIBBS: There are four of them: three girls and one boy.

COVEY: Why are they kept here in jail?

GIBBS: We are trying to have them released. They are in the care of Mrs. Pendleton, the wife of the jailer. (*Going.*) Let me get them.

KABBA SEI[5]: Are you the one who will take us back?

COVEY: No. I am here to act as your interpreter. To speak your story to the whitemen during your trial.

FULIWA: What trial?

COVEY: There were men killed. You are to be tried for murder and piracy.

SENGBE: (*Furious.*) But that was war.

COVEY: What is war for you is only the triangle for them.

BURNAH: But we even spared the Spaniards lives, to sail out of their triangle.

FULIWA: And even so we failed, for we could not sail the ship.

COVEY: Why didn't you follow the stars?

SENGBE: I followed the sun. (*Covey smiles.*) If I had followed the stars, we would have made the return?

COVEY: Then the Spaniards wouldn't have been able to trick you. Whitemen use knowledge to trick. (*Pause.*) I don't say it is good or bad, it simply is; moreover, they change the rules on us all the time. The very basics by which you, Sengbe, and your men judge honor or war or dignity does not exist here. I am not only your interpreter, I am your brother and somehow will teach you how to deal with whitemen.

SENGBE: We thank you.

COVEY: Know this today: a Black man is not allowed to make mistakes because you are never forgiven. They kill you. (*They look at* Covey, *nodding their heads. The* Children *enter, followed by* Gibbs *and* Mrs. Pendleton. *The children run to* Sengbe. *As the lights fade out they begin to chant.*)

End of Movement.

MOVEMENT II

LOWER COURT TRIAL

JUDSON: Are you ready to proceed on the capital charge of murder and piracy?

PROSECUTION-HOLABIRD: The government is prepared to proceed.

STAPLES: We will argue self-defense.

PROSECUTION-HOLABIRD: I call Antonio Ferrer.

SENGBE: Whiteman dog.

COVEY: Don't judge harshly, Sengbe.

The *Amistad* Revolt

ANTONIO: I was there from when it all started to now. Ramon Ferrer the captain was my master. (*Sobs.*) Cinqué killed Ramon Ferrer with a cane knife. I saw it with my eyes. The cook, Celestino, was killed first, killed with a cane knife. I don't know who killed the cook. These Negroes were loose—not chained, they came on us, led by him, him. (*Hysterical.*) He was shouting kill the whiteman—kill the whiteman. (*Crying.*) In the morning they threw the bodies of Celestino and Captain Ferrer over into the sea.

HOLABIRD: Were the captives badly treated?

ANTONIO: They were fed rice, potatoes, bananas, crackers, and meat. They had plenty to eat.

HOLABIRD: Go on.

ANTONIO: (*Haltingly.*) The cook told them we were going to kill them and eat them. I don't know why he told them that, but I know he was joking. The cook did not speak African. He just made signs with hands.

HOLABIRD: Who did you say killed the captain?

ANTONIO: Cinqué.

STAPLES: Did your master, Captain Ferrer, whip the captives?

ANTONIO: I did not see them whipped. What I know is that after they took over the ship, they tied me and Montez and Ruiz. Cinqué was going to kill us.

STAPLES: Will 'War Road' also known as James Covey, take the stand? Mr. Covey, could you tell us what you know of Joseph Cinqué and the others?

COVEY: (*Shivering with ague.*) All these Africans are from Africa. They all have Mende names and their names have meanings. Kale means Bone; Fuliwa means Big Sun. Some of them speak Temne, Kissi, Bullom; but most of them are native speakers of the rivers and mountains on the Guinea Coast that I know. They all agree as to where they sail from: Lomboko.

HOLABIRD: James, how did you learn English?

COVEY: I am a British subject from Sierra Leone, and my name is Covey. Mr. James Covey.

HOLABIRD: Yes! Yes, James, you must understand that in this country we call Negroes by their first names.

COVEY: I am a seaman on Her Royal Majesty's man o' war the *Buzzard*, on which I am addressed as Mr. Covey, Sir.

HOLABIRD: Who is paying you, James?

COVEY: (*Trembling with both ague and anger.*)

HOLABIRD: Did you understand the question, James. Who is paying you to interpret for the Amistad captives?

COVEY: (*Protesting.*) Your honor, I have the right to be addressed in this court by my name and surname. Unless I am so addressed, I refuse to answer. I cannot answer to a first name that could be any person's.

HOLABIRD: Your Honor, James is wasting the court's time. It is irrelevant as to how I address a Negro.

Judson: (*Ordering.*) Please answer the question.

COVEY: No one is paying me. My Commander offered my good services to the Amistad Committee as a gesture of solidarity between the British Navy and the captured Africans. (*Sarcastically.*) William, sir. (*General laughter.*) (*Covey shaking with ague.*)

HOLABIRD: Mr. Covey's *Buzzard* did not capture the *Amistad*. The British Court of Mixed Commissioners has no jurisdiction here except in cases of capture on the sea. I would submit your Honor that he is entitled to no special consideration as witness. Witness dismissed.

STAPLES: I call Sengbe Pieh, also known as Joseph Cinqué to take the stand.

JUDSON: James, please explain to him what an oath is and ask him to tell the truth, the whole truth, and nothing but the truth.

SENGBE: I swear by Gewoh.

COVEY: He swears by God.

JUDSON: Cinqué, do you swear by your God, Gewoh and on the White man's medicine to tell the truth, the whole truth, and nothing but the truth?

The *Amistad* Revolt

SENGBE: I swear by Gewoh.

JUDSON: Go ahead.

SENGBE: I was captured on War Road with my brother-in-law. We were returning from a palaver which I had won. (*Outward emotion.*) I never sold myself. I am married and I have a son. And now perhaps a daughter or another son. We all came in the same house that swims, except for the children, who joined us on the *Amistad*. We were kidnapped separately by Kroomen, Black men, some by Spaniards attacking our towns and burning our houses, shooting and killing with their fire-belching sticks. Seven hundred of us left Lomboko on a ship the *Teçora*. We were kept in iron, hand and feet chained together. (Sengbe *starts to demonstrate their ordeal.*) All the women died, lots of children and men died. Some suffocated, others committed suicide, jumping overboard. Many beaten and wounded and gone mad. In Havana, Ruiz, Montez come to "FEEL" me. Ruiz feel me. (*Touching himself and saying with appreciation, imitating Ruiz. His face and body speak disgust.*) Fine! Fine! Fine! Fine!

Cross fade (A Spanish song is sung as the auction proceeds.)

Flashback (The slave market in Havana. They are led to a raised stage. Don Montez *and* Ruiz, *accompanied by* Antonio.)

MONTEZ: (*To* Antonio.) Let him do a Mende dance. (*Pointing to* Sengbe.)

ANTONIO: (*Making faces and gestures.*) Dance. Dance. *(He demonstrates. Claps his hands.* Sengbe *spits.* Ruiz *raises his whip but is stopped by* Montez.)

MONTEZ: Move there! Move! Move! (Fuliwa *attempts to escape. He is caught and brought back on to the raised stages, where the others have been assembled. The auction is already in progress.*)

SALESMAN: Now! Now! Now! What have we here from darkest Africa? Strong and young and healthy; not more than seventeen years old . . . Am I bid three hundred dollars? Fine, fine ebony Mandinka. Yes! Yes! Do I hear four hundred? Yes sir, four hundred fifty . . . six hundred, six hundred twice, thrice. Going! Going, gone. Sold. (Sengbe *is pushed*

to the front. *He is examined thoroughly by* Montez *with* Ruiz's *approval.*)
... Look at this ... look at this good and strong, very athletic body ready for the plantation ... Am I bid seven hundred? Yes! Yes! Do I hear say eight hundred and fifty? Nine hundred ... nine hundred fifty, twice, thrice ... going ... going, gone and sold ... (*He turns to the children who are now being pushed forward.*)

SALESMAN: Well! Well! Well! Young and tender, fresh from the jungle ... what do you bid? What do you bid? These are a life-time investment. Take ... Take ... do I hear two hundred—two hundred ... She will be a good breeder ... Two hundred fifty ... three hundred ... three hundred ... three hundred ... going ... going ... gone.

VOICE OVER: I grant permission, June 22nd and June 26th 1839 to carry forty-nine Black adults and four children. Ladinos names: Antonio, Simeon, Lucas, Jose, Pedro, Martin, Manuel, Andres, Eduardo, Celedonio, Bartolo, Ramon, Augustin, Evaristo, Casimiro, Melchor, Gabriel, Satorion, Es Colastino, Pascual, Estanislao, Nicholas, Thomas, Salustiano, Francisco, Hipolito, Benito, Vicente, Apoloneo, Leon, Julio, Zenon, Tibureo, Venancio, Luis, Cosme, Usidor, Felipe, Epifaneo, Frederiro, Dionision, Julian, Esteban, Ladislao, Esguiel, Desiderio, Celestino, Bartolo, Gabriel, all property of Don Ruiz and Don Montez to Puerto Principe, by sea. They must present themselves to the respective territorial judge with this permit. Signed Espeleta on the authority of Her Catholic Majesty Isabella of Spain.

Duty, two seals affixed. (*Endorsed.*) Commander of Matriculas.

Let pass in the schooner *Amistad*, to Guanaja, Ferrer, Master. Havana, June 27th, 1839.

In the Courtroom.

STAPLES: This is preposterous! Scandalous! The decree, the decree of Spain of 1817 prohibits the slave trade after 1820 and declares all slaves newly imported from Africa F.R.E.E. (*Shouts.*)

SENGBE: On the *Amistad* we had very little to eat and to drink. We suffered and Ruiz tell the sailors to beat and they beat us bad.

The *Amistad* Revolt

HOLABIRD: Did Don Pedro Montez beat you?

SENGBE: No. But the captain and cook whipped us and the cook was wicked. Very wicked.

HOLABIRD: What about the revolt?

SENGBE: Storm! Storm! Storm everywhere. We broke our chains, we found cane knives and freed ourselves. I killed the cook. The captain killed two of my men. He wounded two more of my men. I killed him and took over the ship. Two sailors jumped overboard. I fed everyone. I put Sessi on the wheel. I left Ruiz and Montez in the slave hold. They cried, they begged, but I told them fetters good enough for Black men, good enough for whitemen. (*Shouts.*) Give us free.

Judgement.

JUDSON: On the 23rd day January AD 1840, upon answers of the Negroes and the Representations of the District Attorney of the United States, this court, having fully heard the parties, do find that the respondents, severally answering as aforesaid, are each of them natives of Africa, and were born free, and ever since have been, and still of right are free, and not slaves; that they were never domiciled in the Island of Cuba, or the dominions of the Queen of Spain, or subject to her laws thereof; that they were severally kidnapped in their native country, in violation of their own rights, were unlawfully held as slaves; that the respondents or some of them, influenced in their desire of recovering their liberty and of returning to their families and kindred in their native country, took possession of the schooner *Amistad*.

And this court doth further find that since the Africans were put on board the schooner to hold the Africans as slaves; that at the time when Cinqué and others, he, making answer, were imported from Africa into the dominion of Spain, there was a law of Spain prohibiting such importation, declaring the person so imported to be free. This law was inforce when the claimants took the possession of the said Africans and put them on board said schooner, and the same has ever been inforce. Therefore, on behalf

of the United States, by virtue of the process issued from this court,
I decree that they may be delivered to the President of the United
States to be transported to Africa. It is so decreed that the Africans
libeled and claims (excepting Antonio Ferrer) be delivered to the
President of the United States to be by his agents transported home
to Africa.

Hammers on desk and leaves.

STAPLES: What do I hear? What do I hear? Judson sets these poor,
unfortunate, helpless, tongueless, defenseless Africans free to
be delivered to the president of America, Mr. Van Buren, to be
transported by his agents to Africa. Africa? Is Judson ignorant of the
secret orders of Mr. President?

PROSECUTION-HOLABIRD: The United States, in pursuance of a demand made
upon them by the duly accredited minister of Her Catholic Majesty,
the Queen of Spain, to the United States, moves to appeal from the
whole and every part of the said decree, except part of the same in
relation to the slave Antonio, to the Circuit Court of Connecticut.

STAPLES: I move for the Africans, by their African names, that so much of
the decree of the district court as relates to them severally may
be dismissed because the United States does not claim them, nor
have they ever claimed any interest in the appellees, respectively,
or either of them, and have no right, either by the law of nations
or by the constitution or laws of the United States, to appear in
the court of the United States, to institute or prosecute claims to
property in behalf of the subjects of the Queen of Spain, under the
circumstances appearing on the record in this case; much less to
enforce the claims of the subjects of a foreign government, to the
persons of the said appellees, respectively, as slaves.

JUDSON: I refuse the motion. I affirm the decree of the district court.

PROSECUTION-HOLABIRD: I then claim in pursuance of a demand made upon
me by the minister of Her Catholic Majesty, the Queen of Spain, to
move an appeal from the whole and every part of the decree of the
court to the Supreme Court of the United States, to be beholden in
the Supreme Court of the United States.

The *Amistad* Revolt

JUDSON: Allowed.

COVEY: What is this?

BRAITHWAITE: Undoing the trial. Holabird has appealed the decision to the United States Supreme Court on behalf of the President.

GIBBS: And Judson allowed it.

VIVIAN: Are you surprised? 'Pares cum paribus facillime at congregantur.'

COVEY: What does it mean?

VIVIAN: It means, James, birds of the same feather flock together, and also that the story of the Amistad Africans has just started.

COVEY: I cannot translate that to them: you will have to get someone else.

GIBBS: There is no someone else. No one they trust, except you.

VIVIAN: War Road, it is your duty. You owe it to them.

SENGBE: (*In agony.*) Elonga ko hui koe hui. (*The other Africans join in.*)

CHORUS: We are dying. We are dying. They are going to kill us.

PENDLETON: Africa? (*Laughs.*) Back to jail. You ain't goin' nowhere, Cinqué.

In the Jail.

COVEY: You will be prosecuted from now on, not by Ruiz or Montez or by those greedy mercenaries, Green, Gedney, and the Spanish minister, but by America.

BRAITHWAITE: It is America that will not set you and your people free.

VIVIAN: From murderer and savage, you have become a liberator; a revolutionary. Do you understand what that means, Sengbe?

BRAITHWAITE: Even though you remain the same Sengbe Pieh or Joseph Cinqué as they have named you: you have become an IDEA. You have made war, so your every action is now the anxious concern for EVERY WHITE. You are a threat and another Nat Turner.

VIVIAN: Your name and image is everywhere. The jailhouse has become a zoo where the public pays to come and look at you.

COVEY: They have your face in portraits and wax. Pendleton is fast becoming a very rich jailer.

BRAITHWAITE: You are the cause for the great debate now between white men who believe that all Black men should be slaves and white men who believe no Black men should be slaves.

COVEY: And that is very dangerous.

VIVIAN: For you to choose to be whatever you want, makes absolutely no difference to them; they see only what they wish to see; your color. Nothing more.

COVEY: This country is obsessed with it and the people, most of them, are racists. They have forgotten that not so long ago, they were a hunted, hounded, pursued, and persecuted people. Homeless and desolate.

VIVIAN: You have been thrown in the great divide of America, Sengbe.

SENGBE: Who can we trust? Who?

FULIWA: Are your friends fighting for something else that we don't know; though you say it is for us you are fighting?

BRAITHWAITE: What do you mean? (Fuliwa *smiles and keeps quiet.*) ... A man can never be a slave if he doesn't know he's a slave. You Sengbe, you are a man apart from this country because you are not lost: you have brought the essence of another continent with you intact, undiluted, pure, free. You frighten. You are frightening because you are still attached to your ancestors. You have an identity, a lineage.

Fade to Van Buren's office.

VOICE: (*Cynically.*) Mr. President, who is what in this case? Here I have in my hand an irate letter from the Spanish Ambassador, Angel Calderón de la Barca, Minister Plenipotentiary of Her Catholic Majesty Isabella of Spain, as well as two plaintive messages from Connecticut District Attorney William Holabird, a threatening letter from the three abolitionist lawyers—Theodore Sedgwick, Seth Staples, and Roger Baldwin—hired by the self-styled Amistad

The *Amistad* Revolt

Defense Committee, and an angry editorial by the editor/poet John Greenleaf Whittier, and a sheaf of newspaper clippings from every part of the country.

VAN BUREN: I suppose that all eyes are on New Haven and not on . . .

FORSYTH: Well, Mr. President, the image of the man you have in your hands is the leading African, Joseph Cinqué or Sinqua, or at least that's the name given to him by the newspapers and the Spaniards.

VAN BUREN: (*Looking at the press cutting.*) And the letter from Holabird?

FORSYTH: He says except the Negroes can be disposed of, he will have to bring them to trial. He also says, should you have any instructions on the subject, he would like to receive them.

VAN BUREN: What is your opinion and assessment of the situation?

FORSYTH: Baldwin, Sedgwick, and Staples argued that neither according to law of the United States nor of Spain can the pretended owner of these Africans establish any legal title to them as slaves. They put the matter on the Spanish law and affirm that Ruiz and Montez have no claim whatever under the treaty of 1795. These Negroes, they say, have only obeyed the dictates of self-defense, and liberated themselves from illegal constraint.

STAPLES: (*Pleading.*) Mr. President, we pray you to submit the case of the Amistad captives for adjudication to the tribunal of the land. We pray that their fate may not be decided in the recesses of the cabinet, where these innocent men can have no counsel and can produce no proof, but in the Halls of Justice with the safeguards that she throws around the persecuted and the oppressed.

FORSYTH: (*Interrupting.*) Mr. President, Mr. President. I have a letter from his Excellency Angel Calderón de la Barca, the Spanish Ambassador, as theatrical as his name— He's demanding that the *Amistad* be immediately delivered up to her owner with every article found on board at the time of her capture, including the Negroes, without payment being exacted for salvage. He claims that no tribunal in the United States has the right to institute proceedings against, or impose penalties upon, the subjects of Spain for crimes committed on board a Spanish vessel and in the waters of Spanish territory. He demands that the Negroes be conveyed to Havana to be tried by the Spanish laws which they have violated.

STAPLES: (*Informing.*) Insurrection in Spanish law is a capital offence, punished by breaking the neck, using a garrote— an iron collar tightened by screw— before being burned at the stake.

FORSYTH: The Ambassador, Mr. President, warned that any delay in the delivery of the vessel and slaves should be indemnified for injury accrued to them. In return Her Catholic Majesty agrees to concede that for the protection of United State property, slaves that have escaped to Cuba will be extradited.

VAN BUREN: And the newspapers.

FORSYTH: Oh damn the newspapers, Mr. President. They have got hold of a wonderful story—the newspapers are drawn along the lines of playing anti-slavery against pro-slavery. They have a jungle prince with his Black pirates of cannibal savages doing the 'hula hula.'

VAN BUREN: And our friend Whittier, of the anti-slavery liberty party?

FORSYTH: My God, the old man calls Cinqué a 'Master Spirit.'

VAN BUREN: And what have you done so far, John?

FORSYTH: I conferred with cabinet members, who agree that the case is covered by the treaty of 1795, articles eight and nine. I answered His Excellency Calderón's letter in the affirmative to that effect. I wrote to William Holabird that he make sure that no proceedings of the circuit court or any other judicial tribunal places the vessel, cargo, or slaves beyond the control of the White House.

VAN BUREN: Men or property, we must keep this under control. We don't want any word getting around that Black slaves have killed white men and tried to sail back to Africa. Think how this could incite in our slaves another Nat Turner.

FORSYTH: The Southern press has been keeping as quiet about it as the Northern press has been noisy. For obvious reasons.

VAN BUREN: Well, slaves aren't supposed to be able to read anyway, John. That's your law.

The *Amistad* Revolt

FORSYTH: There are lots of ways to get around the law ... as you well know. Mr. President, what are your instructions as to how the Negroes are to be disposed of?

VAN BUREN: (*Dictating.*) The Marshal of the United States for the District of Connecticut will deliver over to the Lieutenant John S. Paine of the United States Navy, and aid in his conveying on board the *Grumpus* under his command all the Negroes late of the Spanish schooner *Amistad* under process now pleading before the Circuit Court of the United States. For so doing, this order will be his warrant.

Voice: Given under my hand at the city of Washington, this 7th day of January, AD 1840 by the President's hand.

Flashback to the jail.

JOHN QUINCY ADAMS: (Gibbs *and others standing around.*) Not only is there conspiracy, there is fraud, forgery, withheld evidence, false testimony and perjury.

GIBBS: The *Amistad* passports and other papers, as Dr. Madden pointed out in his testimony, are fraudulent, false documents, obtained illegally from the American consul, Trist, in connivance with the Governor General of Cuba.

BRAITHWAITE: The proceedings on the part of the United States are all wrong from the beginning.

John Quincy Adams: The president has defied Congress by authorizing secret and illegal sailing orders to the *Grumpus*, a U.S. vessel. He has failed to uphold the Constitution by trying to influence the judiciary in violation of the constitutionally decreed separation of the executive powers from the Justice Department.

Vivian: And there is the matter of corruption. The witnesses are lying for money.

GIBBS: (*Laugh.*) Yes! The salvage of the *Amistad*.

JOHN QUINCY ADAMS: What do you think Van Buren is playing at?

GIBBS: He is afraid of the South—pro-slavery.

BRAITHWAITE: He needs the North. It is election year.

JOHN QUINCY ADAMS: (*Pause—looks at them.*) Cinqué has won his trial. The decision has already been taken in the district and circuit courts. What we have to defend now is the *Decision*. This case is not about the abolition of slavery. It is not about acquiring liberty. These men and the children already possess their liberty. They have defended themselves. We must not now confuse the right to liberty with the gift of liberty. This is not a case of emancipation, but of self-defense.

SENGBE: As warriors, we of the *Amistad* will continue the war of the *Amistad*. America will not break our spirits, the whiteman will not sap our will, America will not pervert our memories. We will . . . return to Mendeland.

FULIWA: To our ancestors; Father Siaffa, Kanga, Maada, let it reach you I invoke the spirits of Poro and Sande: these children, let nothing harm them; let them not forget themselves and become slaves converted by trickery to Christianity by Mrs. Pendleton, and then turning them into house slaves. Gewoh, make their bodies strong; let their minds remain in Mende, believing in you, our ancestors. Give them the wisdom to see through the enemy; let them hold themselves in good ways; let them not fall by the wayside; I say let them not fall in love with the evil spirits of our enemies.

BURNAH: (*After a long pause.*) Our teachers have taught us about the road underground that leads to freedom in the North. I say we should escape by this road.

Sengbe: It is not all that simple to escape by that road. Our teachers have also told us how they hang our people on trees and burn them alive.

BURNAH: And, we are not slaves we are warriors.

SESSI: We are warriors.

FULIWA: We are kidnapped Freemen.

SENGBE: And we have memory, we have courage. Through our revolt, we have acquired fortitude, patience, and endurance. We have kept our dignity, though they call us savages and murderers and cannibals.

VIVIAN: Who is the savage? Who is the murderer? They hold us down, their feet on our backs, our faces to the ground, and then they say: we

The *Amistad* Revolt

are ignorant, indolent, and depraved. What haven't they done to us? Everything you can think of has been done to us Blacks. Most northerners say they are opposed to slavery, but they despise Blacks.

SENGBE: We are one in spirit and flesh. We must never betray each other.

COVEY: Inshalahu.

JOHN QUINCY ADAMS: With the blessing of God and if my health permits, I will argue the case before the Supreme Court. (*They all look about themselves, happy and relieved.*) I will implore the almighty God so to control my temper—to enlighten my soul, and to give me utterance that I may prove myself in every respect equal to the task.

Fade out.

Supreme Court People's Adjudicators: Nine empty chairs upstage, cardboard drawing of the Amistad Africans (CUTOUT) are arranged on stage down left center. Kale, the boy captive, is standing behind the cutouts. A mask in silhouette beside him. He is holding a piece of paper from which he reads; but first he reads aloud the 23rd Psalm. John Quincy Adams *enters from stage right. He stops and listens to the voice looking out at the audience. A worried old man.*

KALE: Dear friend Mr. Adams: I want to write a letter to you because you love the Mende people, and you talk to the grand court. We want to tell you one thing. Jose Ruiz and Pedro Montez say we born in Havana, he tells a lie. We stay in Havana ten days and ten nights. We stay no more.[6]

Louisa, *wife of* John Quincy Adams, *enters upper stage left accompanied by* Charles Quincy Adams, *who is accusing his father.*

CHARLES QUINCY ADAMS: Mother, father has really decided to argue the defense of the Amistaders despite my warning. Despite my wishes. It will kill him.

LOUISA: My dearest Charles, I'm sure he's taking into account your wishes and feelings. He has not decided yet.

CHARLES QUINCY ADAMS: You know what this country does to men who love Negroes . . .

LOUISA: Too much.

CHARLES QUINCY ADAMS: Defense in the Supreme Court of Joseph Cinqué will break every opponent he's ever had . . .

LOUISA: . . . and you father has never wanted for enemies or opponents.

CHARLES QUINCY ADAMS: Mother, is he going to spend the rest of his days producing a civil war single-handedly? Does he want to ruin the country just because he . . .

LOUISA: I forbid you to speak of your father in those terms.

CHARLES QUINCY ADAMS: Father should have more consideration for my position in the state legislature and my election.

LOUISA: I am sure your father has no intention of harming your chances at re-election, Charles.

CHARLES QUINCY ADAMS: Of course not intentionally, mother. He just hasn't gotten around to thinking or feeling what it will do to me.

LOUISA: It won't do to you what it will do to those poor men.

CHARLES QUINCY ADAMS: You too, mother!

LOUISA: I only know that the Amistaders must be delivered from the machination of an entire administration that has been set up against their freedom for purely political reasons. They are free men and deserve to go free.

CHARLES QUINCY ADAMS: And we are interfering in the affairs of another government—Spain. We are charging that Cuba is not complying with its treaty with Britain, thus giving her an excuse to walk in and annex it. The Amistaders are the property of Spanish nationals.

LOUISA: (*Shocked.*) Really? THE PROPERTY? Since when are men the property of anyone? Or women?

CHARLES QUINCY ADAMS: Mother you make me sound like I am for slavery and against eventual emancipation. That isn't fair.

The *Amistad* Revolt

JOHN QUINCY ADAMS: (*Angrily.*) Neither is Joseph Cinqué's trial. He has already been set free twice by the Circuit Court of the State of Connecticut.

CHARLES QUINCY ADAMS: (*Pleading.*) Father, the elections are now. And my term is up. Father! You will unseat me in this.

JOHN QUINCY ADAMS: Charles, this has gone beyond simply the freeing of Joseph Cinqué and his men. Even beyond the abolition of slavery. Where the issue WAS the abolition of slavery, it NOW is the right to petition, and the right of free speech. By not allowing the American people the right to petition Congress on the issue of slavery, and by not allowing any discussion of slavery in Congress, we are in direct violation of our most precious treasure, the constitution of the United States. If the House can refuse petitions concerning slavery, why they can refuse petition on ANY issue it wants! Free white Americans are not the issue, Charles; for the first time they are asking if any among us is enslaved are the rest of us free? As for Cinqué, if the White House can interfere with a verdict of the Judiciary, then where is the separation between the two branches dictated by the constitution? Where is Democracy? Where is Justice?

LOUISA: If the Supreme Court doesn't defy him, where are we?

JOHN QUINCY ADAMS: A slave-owning chief justice will NEVER defy a slave-loving president. (Louisa *and* Charles *exit.* Adams *moves upstage to the empty chairs, walking behind them, he stops upstage center.*) . . . While a single remnant of physical power is left to me to write and to speak, the world will retire from me before I shall retire from the world . . . But do I intend to have anything to do with the trial of Joseph Cinqué. (*He smiles to himself. A very rascally and determined smile.*)

KALE: (*Voice echoes.*) Dear Friend Mr. Adams: We want to ask the grand court what we Mendes have done wrong? What for Americans keep us in prison?

JOHN QUINCY ADAMS: May it please you most able adjudicators, I entreat you to regard my argument with understanding especially where I shall perhaps be more likely to exhibit at once the infirmities of age and the inexperience of youth, than to render those services to the individuals whose lives and liberties are at your mercy: to save or condemn them.

As it is not my wish to waste any of your valuable time, I will therefore proceed to the heart of the matter of this case in saying that, I derive, in the distress I feel both for myself and my clients, consolation from two courses—first, that the rights of my clients to their lives and liberties have already been defended by my learned friend and colleague in so able and complete a manner as leaves me scarcely anything to say, and I feel that such full justice has been done to their interests that any fault or imperfection of mine will merely be attributed to its true cause; and secondly, I derive consolation from the thought that this is a court. The people's court of JUSTICE. If this should sound trivial, it is because I believe with all honesty and sincerity, that there will not be any occasions during this hearing for me to ask you, the peoples' adjudicators, to consider what justice is. Justice that has been defined thousands of years ago. Justice as it is felt and understood and practiced by all who understand human relations and human rights.

In a court of justice, where there are two parties present justice demands that the rights of each party should be allowed to himself, as well as that each party has a right to be secured and protected by the court. This observation is important, because I appear here on behalf of thirty-six individuals, but will act on the consideration that the life and the liberty of every one of them must be determined by its decision for himself alone.

I trust that by the time the ultimate decision of this court is established, you, our peoples' adjudicators, will pay due attention to the circumstances and condition of every individual concerned.

They are here individually. The predicament of one is not necessarily the same as and for the other. They are different characters and under different circumstances. In some of the proceedings by which they have been brought into the custody and under the protection of this court, thirty two or three of them have been charged with crime of murder. Three or four of them

The *Amistad* Revolt

are female children, incapable in the judgment of our laws, of the crime of murder or piracy, or perhaps of any other crime.

Yet, from the day when the vessel was taken possession of by one of our naval officers, they have all been held as close prisoners, now for the period of eighteen long months, under the custody and by authority of the courts of the United States.

When I say I take consolation from the consideration that I stand before a court of Justice, I am obliged to take this ground, because, as I shall show, another department of the government of the United States has taken, with reference to this case, the ground of utter injustice, and these individuals for whom I appear, stand before this court, awaiting their fate from its decision, under the array of the whole executive power of this nation against them, in addition to that of a foreign nation. Considering the duty I have to discharge, in which, in supporting the motion to dismiss the appeal, though painful for me, I shall be obliged not only to investigate and submit to the censure of this court, the form and manner of the proceedings of the executive in this case, but the validity and the motive of the reason assigned for its interference in this unusual manner in a suit between parties for their individual rights.

That government is still in power, and thus subject to the control of the court, the lives and liberties of all my clients are in its hands. If I should pass over the course it has pursued, those who have not had the opportunity to examine the case and perhaps the court itself, might decide that nothing improper had been done, and that the parties I represent had not been wronged by the course pursued by the executive . . . the courts of the United States have enslaved the captives of the *Amistad* before they could restore them to their pretended masters. Why?

Flashback.

KALE (*A recording*): Dear friend Mr. Adams. You have children, you have friends, you love them, you feel sorry if Mende people come and carry them all to Africa. We feel bad. Our friends all feel bad for us. Americans don't take us in ship. We on shore and Americans tell us slave ship catch us. They say we make you free. If they make us free they tell true, if they no make us free they tell lie. If American people give us free we glad, if they no give us free we sorry— we worry for Mende people little, we sorry for American people great deal, because God punish liars.

SENGBE: If I could have freed all my men by killing all the whitemen, I would have done it. And if I could have freed all my men by killing none of the whites, I would have done that. As it is, I had to kill two, save two, and leave the rest to sink to the bottom of the sea.

FULIWA: We thought the voyage was ended with the capture of the *Amistad*, but it continues even now.

JOHN QUINCY ADAMS: Why do you say your voyage continues even now?

SENGBE: Because we are not saved.

FULIWA: Ruiz and Montez are saved.

BURNAH: The sea is still here.

SENGBE: When the sea was finished with us it left us by trickery in a land in which we are helpless, despised and captive as on the water.

FULIWA: Nothing has changed except the earth under our feet.

SENGBE: All we see, and feel and hear is rejection and unfeeling hardness, as smooth and careless as the sea from which we rescued ourselves.

Grabeau: Here men circle us like snakes and would eat our hearts if they could. We see it in their eyes. They fear us. And we fear them but they don't know.

FULIWA: This your land Maada Adams is worse than typhoon for Mende. It sweeps away our dignity, our knowledge, cutting our language like cutting off our tongues.

SENGBE: The people of your land demand the death of our souls and this is more than slavery. This trial is to teach us your law and order; but underneath it is a world of hatred, of rejection, of denial of our humanity, and contempt about us except our price.

FULIWA: They have prepared a deep grave or is it a ship to sail us far beyond?

The *Amistad* Revolt

JOHN QUINCY ADAMS: You know you have friends in Tappan, Mr. Baldwin, Rev. Gibbs, Mr. Staples and Mr. Townsend.

SENGBE: They are our friends yes; but their fight is not our fight.

JOHN QUINCY ADAMS: That is not true.

SENGBE: They fight to stop slavery in America for reasons we do not know.

JOHN QUINCY ADAMS: Their fight is your fight and the trial is necessary to determine that acts of violence that took place between you and the Spaniards. It must be proved on which side these acts were right and on which side they were wrong. It is clear to me as to any free man why you revolted, but was it a FEELING or a PLAN? Was it circumstances and change, or was it reasoning? I look on what you tell me as an illumination, not a confession.

SENGBE: How can you speak of confession? A confession of what? How can you speak of right versus wrong or law and lawlessness to someone who has been taken by force, beaten by force, transported by force, sold by force? Please Maada, do not speak of confession to a man who is at war. I have enemies able to take my freedom and my life. I am a prisoner of war. All of us and the children are your country's prisoners of war.

FULIWA: The sea betrayed us; shall the land also betray us?

SENGBE: We will call you MAADA.

JOHN QUINCY ADAMS: M.A.A.D.A.

COVEY: It means grandfather, sir. It is the Mende title of supreme honor; Sire. The medium and link between the past and present, the seer into the future; the venerated one.

JOHN QUINCY ADAMS: I thank you. (*Pause.*) I want you to understand that the judicial system of the United States provides for the right of appeal from a lower court to a higher court . . . understand, you are not being held in slavery, son, but for a trial before . . . before . . . how do you translate the Supreme Court?

COVEY: Council of Paramount Chiefs.

SENGBE: (*Smiles.*) You, too, Maada, President, would be considered a paramount chief in Mendeland, and that means, there is no division between those who rule and those who judge.

JOHN QUINCY ADAMS (*A recording*): In the past two years there had been anti-Black riots in Philadelphia, Boston, New York, and Chicago. The abolitionist, Garrison, had been mobbed, stripped naked and dragged by a rope through the streets of New York—A minister in New Hampshire had been jerked to his knees during an anti-slavery sermon and tried for inciting violence. Free colored people's churches, schoolhouses, and dwellings had been mobbed, sacked, and burned down in Providence, Cincinnati, and Harrisburg. In St. Louis, a slave had been burned to death over a slow fire in a public square, and Elijah Lovejoy, the only newspaper editor who had spoken out against it, has been smoked out of his publishing office and murdered. The message is clear: Negroes and white men who love Negroes are not safe in this land, under this flag . . .

SENGBE: Maada, you say that Mr. Tappan and his friends are our friends and that their fight is our fight. I say no. No because I know and my brothers know and even the children know that: I, Cinqué, as they call me: I am an unclosed case, and for them, we are heathens to be Christianized, I an unwelcome nigger, to be disposed of in any way as soon as possible.

JUDSON: You and your friends have undertaken what you cannot accomplish. These niggers have no place in our continent. They can never ever be integrated. You are fanatical about them. You are violating the constitution of our Republic . . . They belong to Africa.

SENGBE: Maada, how is it possible for a white man to fight for the Black man in this country? It is dangerous for you. Your people will say you are mad. I, Joseph Cinqué, am a reincarnation of Nat Turner, his rebellion, his revolt. Why? I and my brothers must be destroyed just as Nat Turner and his men were destroyed.

JOHN QUINCY ADAMS: Your trial is a conversation between America and Africa, not between the Republic and the slave.

COVEY: Then, Sir, we run the same risk as the first trial in this new one before the Supreme Court.

The *Amistad* Revolt

JOHN QUINCY ADAMS: Yes, but it is most serious, most serious. The warrant the president issued to put Joseph Cinqué on board the *Grumpus* assumed a power that no American president has ever assumed before, one which is questionable if the most despotic government of Europe possessed it. Such a power puts the personal freedom of any citizen of the United States at the disposition of executive discretion, caprice, or tyranny.

KALE: (*Voice in the background.*) Dear friend Mr. Adams: We want you to ask the grand court what we Mendes have done wrong? You have children. You have friends, you love them.

JOHN QUINCY ADAMS: Thank him. Thank him for me. Thank him for his letter. I will try to live up to it, somehow. At his age, one still believes . . . in justice. It is very, very hard to accept anything else.

COVEY: (*Pointedly.*) But Mr. President, you, too, were the president of a slave-holding republic. (*Echoes.*)

JOHN QUINCY ADAMS: (*Silence.*) (*Painfully.*) Ai, I too. (*Pause.*) (*Resolutely.*) There's much in risking one's life for justice.

VOICES: (*Echoing.*) Gracious heavens, John Quincy Adams, you are great in everything else, but you show your weakness on the subject of slavery. Pray what have you to do with the Amistaders?—Do you want your name, your honor and your pride and place to descend to the latest posterity with this BLOT on it: Mr. Adams loves the Negroes too much—UNCONSTITUTIONALLY.

COVEY (*A recording*): (*Echo.*) You, too, were the President of a slave-holding republic.

Fade out.

PROSECUTION (Attorney General Henry D. Gilpin, Holabird): The prosecution presents its argument; that the United States must pursue the course required by the laws of nations and if the court is satisfied, on the first point that there is double proof concerning the property, then this property ought to be delivered so that it may be restored to the Spanish owners. If this be so, the court below has erred, because it has not decreed any part of the property be delivered entire, except the slave Antonio. From the vessel and cargo, it has deducted the salvage, diminishing them by that amount; and the Negroes it has entirely refused to direct to be delivered.

Fade out.

Flashback.

FULIWA: How could a verdict be on trial without the flesh-and-blood people involved?

BURNAH: This is a funny world—America where an idea is more important than a man's life.

SENGBE: (*Joking.*) Is the verdict to be tried by real men or by other verdicts?

Grabeau: I want to go to Washington in chains.

COVEY: They won't let you.

SENGBE: Will they let me attend my own hanging?

FULIWA: They will hang the verdict in Washington, not us.

ANTONIO: (*Crying.*) They will send me back to my owners no matter what they decide. I am the LADINO bastard. They have to return me.

SENGBE: I won't let them. Here we all will die if they try.

ANTONIO: (*Holding fast to Sengbe.*) Save me, Sengbe.

SENGBE: You are one of us. The same spirit, Socora, Socora.

ALL: Wooo—wooo—wooo.

Fade out.

JOHN QUINCY ADAMS: This case does not only affect the destiny of these unfortunate Africans, it involves considerations affecting our national character in the eyes of the civilized world, as well as questions of the power on the part of the government of the United States. It presents for the very first time, the questions

The *Amistad* Revolt

whether the government, which was established for the promotion of JUSTICE, founded on the great principles of the REVOLUTION, as proclaimed in the Declaration of Independence, can consistently become a party to proceedings of the enslavement of human beings cast upon our shores and found in condition of freemen within the territorial limits of a FREE and SOVEREIGN STATE.

I shall appeal to no sectional prejudices, and assume no positions in which I shall not hope to be sustained by intelligent minds from the south as well as from the north. More than a year has elapsed since the decree of the district court denying the title of Ruiz and Montez and pronouncing the Africans free; not a particle of evidence has since been produced in support of their claims. And yet, strange as it may seem, during all this time, not only the sympathy of the Spanish minister, but the powerful aid of our own government, have been enlisted in their behalf. The district court exercises its jurisdiction over the parties and found that the right was with the other party, not in accordance with the impulses of sympathy. And consequently it now appears that everything which has flowed from this mistaken or misapplied SYMPATHY, was wrong from the beginning.

I enquire by what right all this sympathy from Lieutenant Gedney to the Secretary of State, and from the Secretary of State, as it were, to the nation, is to be extended to two Spaniards from Cuba and utterly denied to the fifty-three victims of their lawless violence? By what right is it denied to the men who restored themselves to freedom?

There is no law, statute, or constitution, no code or treaty, applicable to the proceedings of the executive of the Judiciary, except THAT law (*He points to the Declaration of Independence hanging upper stage center*). I know of no other law that reaches that case of my clients, but the law of nature and of nature's God on which our fathers placed our own national existence . . .

Fade into flashback.

KALE: Dear friend Mr. Adams: We want you to know that Mende people think. None of you people believe that Mende people can think.

Mende people have got souls. If court ask who brought Mende people to America...

Fade to Court.

JOHN QUINCY ADAMS: The Africans were in possession, and had the presumptive right of ownership, of the *Amistad*. They were at peace with the United States, and truly, they were not pirates; they were on a voyage to their native home. They had acquired the right and so far as their knowledge extended, they had the power, of prosecuting the voyage; the ship was in the territory of the State of New York and entitled to all the provisions of the law of nations, and the protection and comfort which the laws of that state secure to every human being within its limits. My arguments are based and will show that the proceedings of the United States are all wrong from the beginning...

Cross fade to flashback.

LOUISA: Slaves are jailed and auctioned in our capital. There is a slave market in Washington. There are unnumbered wrongs inflicted on a million of our Black country-women. Have you ever visited a Black slave woman in jail? Have you been down to the Washington jail? Have you ever listened to the tales of sorrow a female slave can tell you, of the unbridled passion of a master? Have you ever cried with a Black widow torn from her assassinated husband, or the Black mother sold away from her children? Can you feel the wrongs of these women and sisters and not hate the system which degrades them to the level of beasts? Can we feel as we should for these unhappy women and not ask in the presence of God: what would Thou have me do in the great work of rooting out slavery from our midst and our land? Joseph Cinqué is only one part of God's plan. That resisted by those who cling to it with energy and desperation and fury as only fiends can summon when they know their hour has come. The end will be slow. Woe to the abolitionists if we dream that our work is well-nigh done. But know this, whatever come of this trial, the cause of anti-slavery and the cause of women's rights are one and the same.

The *Amistad* Revolt

Cross fade to John Quincy Adams.

JOHN QUINCY ADAMS: What combination of ideas led to the conclusion that the President of the United States had the power to decide such cases and to dispose of persons and of property at his own discretion? That the president can issue a proclamation, declaring that no court in this country could hold cognizance of the case. (*Stops to take a breath.*) If the President of the United States has arbitrary power to do it in the case of the Africans, and send them beyond the seas for trial, he could do it by the same authority in the case of American citizens! Would this not disable forever the power of habeas corpus? I say the Africans were here with their ship. The Africans, who had the prima facie title to the *Amistad*, did not bring the vessel into our waters themselves, but were brought here against their wills, by deception. The original voyage from Lomboko in Africa, was continued by the Spaniards in the *Amistad*. Pursuing that voyage was a violation of the laws of offense; the deed begun in Africa was not consummated until the Negroes were landed at their port of final destination in Puerto Principe. The clandestine landing in Havana, the unlawful sale in the barracoons, the shipment on board the *Amistad*, were all parts of the original transaction . . . If the good offices of the president are to be rendered to any proprietors of the shipping in distress, they are due to the Africans. They were brought into our waters by their enemies, who are still seeking to reduce them from freedom to slavery as a REWARD FOR HAVING SPARED THEIR LIVES.

PROSECUTION (*A recording*): May it please the court, the treaty . . .

JOHN QUINCY ADAMS: (*Interrupting.*) The treaty under consideration cannot apply to slaves. It says ships and merchandise. Is that language applicable to human beings? Will this court so affirm? It says they shall be restored entire. Is it a treaty between cannibal nations, that a stipulation is needed for restoration of merchandise entire, to prevent parties for cutting off the legs and arms of human beings before they are delivered up? The sympathy of the executive government; and as it were, of the nation in favor of the slave traders, and against these unfortunate, helpless, tongueless, defenseless Africans . . .

PROSECUTION: (*Shouting.*) May it please the court: Mr. Adams has pushed the argument a step beyond! The appearance of the Africans in the court below is not to be regarded as 'destitute of right' as well as their appearance here. They are dictators, in the form of supplicants, and their suggestions to the court, and their application for its judgment, upon some and important questions of fact are distorted by an ingenious logic which it is difficult to follow. Applications, made without the slightest expression of a wish, except to obtain that judgement, and in a form which, it might be supposed, would secure admission into any court, are repudiated, under the harsh name of executive interference. How can it be justly said that there has been any EXECUTIVE INTERFERENCE?

JOHN QUINCY ADAMS: (*Imitating Spanish accent.*) Gubernativamente: The word used several times in correspondence, that no American translator has been able to translate into our language. It means, "By the simple will of the Executive." That is what it means. I read to you the confidential answer of the Secretary of State (of the 12th of January) to the inquiries of the federal marshal of New Haven, Connecticut. It says: "I have to state by direction of the President, that if the decision of the court is such as is anticipated (that is, that the captives should be delivered up as slaves) the ORDER OF THE PRESIDENT shall be carried into execution, unless as appeal shall actually have been interposed. And if on the contrary the decision of the court is different, you are to take out an appeal, and allow things to remain as they are until the appeal shall have been decided." The very phraseology of this instruction is characteristic of its origin, and dispenses the Secretary of State from the necessity of stating that it emanated from the PRESIDENT himself. The inquiry of the marshal was barefaced enough; whether, if the executive warrant and the judicial decree came into conflict, he should obey the president, or the judge? No! says the Secretary of State. If the decree of the judge should be in our favor, and you can steal a march upon the Negroes by foreclosing their right to appeal, ship them off without mercy and without delay and if the decree should be in their favor, do not fail to enter an instantaneous appeal to the Supreme Court where the chances are more hostile to self-emancipated slaves.

The *Amistad* Revolt

PROSECUTION: BOO. RUBBISH.

JOHN QUINCY ADAMS: Was ever such a scene of Lilliputian trickery enacted by the rulers of a great, magnanimous and Christian nation? Contrast it with that act of self-emancipation by which the savage, heathen barbarians Cinqué, Fuliwa, and Grabeau liberated themselves and their suffering fellow countrymen. This review of all the proceedings of the Executive I make with the utmost pain, because it is necessary to bring it fully before you, to show that the course of that department has been dictated, throughout, not by JUSTICE but by SYMPATHY— and a SYMPATHY most partial and unjust. And this sympathy prevailed to such a degree, among all the persons concerned in this business, as to have perverted their minds to all the most sacred principles of law and right, on which the liberties of the people of the United States are founded. This court should decide only on consideration of all the rights, both natural and social, of EVERY ONE of these individuals. I have endeavored to show that they are entitled to their liberty from this court. These Negroes had a right to assert their liberty. My argument in behalf of the captives of the *Amistad* is CLOSED.

Fade out.

SENGBE: (*The call.*) Am I a good man or have I committed some unpardonable sin in this life or another which renders me unfit to live? Have I brought the trial and slavery upon myself in some mysterious way, or has the whiteman imposed it upon me unjustly? The whiteman has no power over me even if he kills me and burns my body.

FULIWA: We were snatched away from everything we know and love.

SENGBE: This new world has nothing to offer me. They have turned me into a new person never to be the same again (*Trembling and in tears.*), even if I return. (Fuliwa *goes to him trying to console him.*) I may have killed, but I have also died—Ah Gewoh. Gewoh.

Fade out.

VOICE (*A recording*): The decree of the circuit and the district court is upheld, including the restitution of Antonio Ferrer to Cuba and his legal master Ramon Ferrer, and except so far as it directs the Negroes to be delivered to the President, to be transported to Africa. As to this, it is reversed. The said Negroes are declared to be free and go without delay. (*Rejoicing.*)

GIBBS: May the blessing, of those ready to perish fall on you.

JOHN QUINCY ADAMS: Glorious. Glorious not only as a triumph of humanity, but as a vindication of the American national character from reproach and dishonor.

LOUISA: It is great relief, Mr. Adams, that your cause is settled and well settled.

JOHN QUINCY ADAMS: I was pleading for more, much more, than my own life, Mrs. Adams.

Fade out.

The Call.

The Amistaders *are sitting together quietly.* Covey *enters laughing and happy.*

COVEY: The Paramount Chiefs have set you free. (*An explosion of joy.*) President Maada Adams won a great victory in the court and then left without saying goodbye.

SENGBE: We can say goodbye to him before we sail. And we can sail tomorrow.

ALL: We sail tomorrow—tomorrow.

COVEY: You don't have the *Amistad*, Sengbe. The award of the *Amistad* as salvage to Lieutenant Gedney, is upheld. We don't know how to get you and your men home.

SENGBE: (*Showing no emotion.*) And the President, are we still under his custody?

COVEY: No. That too has been removed. You and your men are no longer in the custody of the President. You are immediately and forthwith a free man. (*A pause. Tension as the captives look from one to another.*) (*Gibbs, Braithwaite, Vivian and Others enter happily, shouting.*) You are free—free—free.

SENGBE: I thank American men. I thank American men.

From the distance, church bells begin to ring. A cannon is fired. The Amistaders break into singing and dancing, joined by the others. Covey *and* Vivian *move to an isolated corner and continue what seem to be the beginning of a "getting to know you" love dialogue through dance.* Sengbe *goes into a dreamlike reunion with* Baya Bia *and* Tau. Fuliwa *is engrossed happily with the* Children. Braithwaite *watches his daughter jealously from the distance.* Gibbs *reads from his pocket Bible.* Antonio *pleads with* Grabeau *and* Burnah *to take him with them.* John Quincy Adams *and* Louisa *watch happily from a distance.* Charles Quincy Adams, *despairing, is standing with* Montez, Ruiz, Judson, *etc. The* Egugu *mask enters and all freeze.* Maada *moves toward the mask.*

MAADA: (*To the mask.*) The war is over. We are free. Free to leave. Free to starve. Free to rot.

Blackout.

The Broken Handcuff

BY RAYMOND E. D. DE'SOUZA GEORGE

Dedicated to

(Millicent, Elvina, Illia, and Raymond)

MY FAMILY

PART ONE

Scene One	Burial Rites
Scene Two	The Village Square
Scene Three	Independence beyond the Grave
Scene Four	Life in the Village
	The Sun and the Moon in Combat (Eclipse)
	The Next Morning
	Capture

PART TWO

Scene One	In Transit from Lomboko
Scene Two	The Mutiny
Scene Three	The Trials
Scene Four	Return—Disillusionment—Death and Burial

People in the Play

Mourners
Kakpindi
Lavalie
Well-Dressed Man
First Native
Second Native
Third Native
Slaves
Governor
Bai Bureh
Mammy Yoko
Akunna
Calendar
Sir Milton
Sengbe

Burnah
Grabo
First Hunter
Second Hunter
Whiteman
Sailor
Abolitionist
Judge Smith Thompson
Women
Man
Judge Judson
Quincy Adams
Attendant
Judge Taney
Pastor

PART ONE—SCENE ONE

BURIAL RITES (IMPROVISED)

Painted or made up, a giant handcuff stands against the back wall. The stage is littered with dry leaves and symbols of slavery. A shot is heard off-stage as the curtains/lights reveal a Group of Mourners *mostly crouching around a grave at centre stage. They sing funeral dirges as the burial rites draw to a close. The rites concluded, the* Mourners *go out in different directions leaving* Two Men *shoveling earth over the grave, while the third (*Lavalie*), stands in a supervisory stance. They finish the exercise and go out very slowly. Tempo builds up again. Years later,* Lavalie *and* Kakpindi *enter, the latter with a shovel and brooms. Scene two begins.*

PART ONE—SCENE TWO

THE VILLAGE SQUARE

KAKPINIDI: (*As they enter.*) But eh, dakpe, you don't expect an elder to do things like that when there are little children in the home.

LAVALIE: That is exactly what I am talking about—the convenient shifting of expectations. Nobody expects to be doing anything when somebody else could do it. In some countries this type of behaviour is science. They just sit and wait; they stare and wait; they wait and wait and wait until patience becomes impatient with them—

KAKPINIDI: But dakpe, what can we do?

A Well-Dressed Man *enters, counting money.* Two Natives *pushing a third who is pleading.*

FIRST NATIVE: Keep quiet and sit down. (Lavalie *sits.*) Look there dakpe benyama!

THIRD NATIVE: For God's sake dakpe, don't do it—No dakpe, don't give me away.

SECOND NATIVE: Give you away? Free! No, we are going to sell you.

THIRD NATIVE: Please don't sell me off. Dakpe, I am your brother.

SECOND NATIVE: Please don't you want to go for me? A brother must sacrifice himself for his people as willingly as you are doing. (*By now they are centre stage. They strike a bargain with the* Well-Dressed Man.) I shall tell the village how happy you were to do your duty. (*They celebrate greedily and turn to go.*)

THIRD NATIVE: My brothers! My fathers! (*The* Well-Dressed Man *begins to pull him away.*) O my mother! People of my hometown, can't you hear me?

KAKPINDI: O Ngewo! Lavalie, is this thing happening all the time?

LAVALIE: What do you think I brought you out here for? If you have forgotten yourself I will remind you—Even if a broom is mistaken for a toy by a small boy, I am sure a man of your age is aware of its function—Hurry up! (*He begins to sweep.*)

KAKPINDI: Lavalie, the mind is willing but the body is weak.

LAVALIE: That is how much of our history and culture were swept away. Weak bodies can be motivated by willing minds. The drummers would not like the rustling leaves to dilute their rhythm, nor would the dancers want their soles to be pricked by thorns. (*Quickens his pace.*) That is the spirit. Maybe I should get some more men to help you. (*Hands brooms to two members of the audience. Thanks them in Mende when they finish.*) That is what we call constructive—. (*Chokes. Pours libation silently.*) Let the drum of the Lion Mountains come out—and let the drummers, singers, dancers combine in harmony as they experience their innate African sense of rhythm—Let the drums roll! (*No response.*) My people. (*To the audience.*) I fear for our children. We fought for freedom—then used the freedom to sell our brothers, our fathers, out mothers, our wives, sons and —all we had. Even the things that make us what we are. We killed ourselves in those sales and are still killing our heroes with dishonour.

PEOPLE: I ala koto mymu! A koto bekithon, I ala koto maynu!

LAVALIE: Yes! Thank you. Ridicule! That is the usual epitaph we ascribe to the memory of valiant sons of the soil. Those worthy sons we neglect as we bask in our chronic aura of nationalistic indifference and ignorance.

The Broken Handcuff

PEOPLE: He was truly a great man. A brave trade unionist and an utterly fearless leader of men.

LAVALIE: I totally forgot that. Lip servicing. Mouthing borrowed linguistic tokens which the Yelibas and Yelimusus cannot translate. (*A slave train enters.*) Those are men of courage who will never know how truly courageous they were in their sacrifice. They experienced the reality of living death through ignominy of feeling and sometimes even accepting that they were less than human in the eyes of their fellow men. Is it any different among ourselves today?

PEOPLE:
Mama e!	Pingila!
Papa e!	Pingila!
Mama e! Papa e!	Pingila!
Wi de na wi os	Pingila!
Wi no ambɔg nɔbɔdi[1]	Pingila!
Ɛnjɔy wi fam dɛm	Pingila!
Ɛnjɔy dɛn pikin	Pingila!
Ɛn wetin Gɔd gi wi	Pingila!
Siknɛs bin de	Pingila!
Bɔt mɛrɛsin sɛf de	Pingila!
So wɛl bodi	Pingila!
No bin de fɔ we	Pingila!
Tin dɛn bin de	Pingila!
Fɔ it, fɔ drink, fɔ wɛr	Pingila!
Fridɔm bin de	Pingila!
Fridɔm bin de	Pingila!
Bɔt wan-tɛm wan-tɛm	Oya!
Sɔn trenja dɛn kam	Oya!
Dɛn miksop sɔn wi broda dɛm	
Dɛn miksop sɔn wi broda dɛm	Oya!
Mek tings ful dɛn yay	Oya!
It ful dɛn yay	Oya!
Klos ful dɛn yay	Oya!
Rɔm tɔn dɛn ed	Oya!
Kɔpɔ tɔn dɛn ed	Oya!
I ton dɛn ed	Oya!
I twis dɛn at	Oya!

      E mama e!   Pingila!
      E papa e!   Pingila!

      Dɛn bigin tɛk wi go   Wan bay wan!
      Wi respɛkt fɔ wi sɛf   Dɛn kil ɔl tin. (*Freeze.*)

LAVALIE: Are those the reasons we lack self-esteem—we lack a sense of identity—we gullibly embrace all those things which are constantly telling us we are a people without roots—without heroes— without pride? Why did they endure all that? If the courage of some of those we send to the world beyond—some of those we condemn to a living-hell—some whose apparent unworthiness shame our assumed virtues—if only their courage and greatness could have been frozen so that when the lights go out they thaw and flow in rivulets of hope?—But alas!—Yet there could still be a glimmer of hope. Even history is willing to, and can teach when a people learn to listen and act.

PEOPLE: If you will die
            Die fighting to be free
     You will kill
            You will kill for your freedom.
     If you will kill
            You will kill to be free
            Then you will die
            For your freedom
            You will die!

The lights go down.

PART ONE—SCENE THREE
INDEPENDENCE BEYOND THE GRAVE

Actors come on in very low lights with crosses bearing inscriptions of their names indicating gravestones.[2] *They freeze behind the crosses. As the lights come up we hear singing by the people. (Possibly recorded.) At the end the freeze is broken.*

The Broken Handcuff

PEOPLE: We raise up our hearts and our voices on high the hills and the valleys reecho our cry firmly united, ever we stand singing thy praise O native land.

GOVERNOR: Should any person have any wicked thought in his heart or do anything knowingly to disturb the peace and comfort of this our colony, let him be rooted out, O God, from off the face of the Earth, but have mercy upon him hereafter.[3]

BAI BUREH: I do not like the expression 'our colony' but I really do appreciate the thought and concern you seem to have for my people.

GOVERNOR: You people are my people also. God gave me a divine burden for your country.

BAI BUREH: You carried your burden well, but only up to a point.

GOVERNOR: How?

BAI BUREH: You pretended to be philanthropic, but your people have drastically changed the tone of your feelings for my people. You cleverly imposed your own way of life, your dress, the way you talk and even—

GOVERNOR: But has it not been good for our country?

BAI BUREH: Your country? Yes!!

GOVERNOR: I am talking about your own people, people entrusted to my care, together, our—

MAMMY YOKO: Well, it has not been good. Our people learned to deceive. They have become treacherous and untrustworthy. They are now greedy, they compete to see who will covet what and covet most. Avarice is now one of their primary virtues.

GOVERNOR: These are vices you find in human beings everywhere.

MAMMY YOKO: You should have left them as they were.

GOVERNOR: I am sure we only wanted to do our best for you.

AKUNNA: You may be right, but I suspect your kindness was induced by the generous returns you expected to reap from our lands. It was a cover to devastate the culture, heritage and resources of our people.

You made the bulk of our people look down on things that used to hold them together as people.

GOVERNOR: That was not what we expected—

AKUNNA: That was more your intention rather than your expectation.

GOVERNOR: However, you will agree that the things we passed on have given you an international perspective and outlook.

BAI BUREH: Indeed! But it has undermined and totally destroyed any sense of nationality and what is genuinely our own.

CALENDAR: Faya! Faya! Faya! Faya! Faya de kam!
              A want to si mi loving gyal,
              Loving gyal a love so well,
              Faya! Faya! Faya! Bebi o,
              Faya de kam!

SIR MILTON: Thank you, Mr. Calendar. Even when our hearts are hot and angry and our tongues quick, our culture tells us that love still has a place in the human heart. Gentlemen, let us allow peace to prevail as we reminisce.

GOVERNOR: If you'll excuse me, lady and gentlemen—

SIR MILTON: I hope Your Excellency is not terribly disturbed by the candid views we expressed as we reminisce.

GOVERNOR: Well, I had no reason being here in the first place.

AKUNNA: You have, Your Excellency, you have. Remember, God gave you a divine burden.

Calendar: Your Excellency Sir, my brother don't mean to make you annoyed but the truth is the truth, and the truth is that—

GOVERNOR: The truth is that the present is an indication that your people have come a long way.

SIR MILTON: Indeed!

AKUNNA: A very very long way down the line.

GOVERNOR: Because they have discarded the good things which we taught them.

The Broken Handcuff

AKUNNA: Naturally, because they had been forced to discard the even better values which they had been used to long before your disruptive arrival.

GOVERNOR: I don't agree with you, Sir. Excuse me, what is your name?

AKUNNA: Isaac Theophilous Akunna Wallace-Johnson.

BAI BUREH: And what is your own name?

GOVERNOR: Governor Clarkson.

BAI BUREH: So you are Clarkson? I have heard a lot about a farewell address you made. But I am surprised that you disagree with what my brother has just said.

GOVERNOR: I certainly do because . . .

AKUNNA: If you do, do you like what you see happening now?

GOVERNOR: Of course I don't, but—

MAMMY YOKO: You do! He does! His people are now comfortably placed to use the tools that are now on the shelves and that has always been their intention. Their plan has never changed, but some of us are slow to see it.

BAI BUREH: Yoko, you are right. Either by subtlety, coercion or trickery, his people have always been makers and users of tools.

GOVERNOR: Gentlemen, your views have come as a very big surprise—a great shock to me—

SENGBE: (*Breaks his silence.*) Just as your presence here surprised me—Brothers and sister, I think the Governor has run out of time and words. His continued stay will be a distraction. He should be allowed to go.

GOVERNOR: God knows our intention has always been honourable. (*As he leaves.*) You will have reason to think again about some of the things I prayed about.

He goes—PAUSE.

SENGBE: Well!—We have been setting our eyes on the wrong targets all the time. When the stranger arrived he took our attention. We were distracted. When he was going did he ask us to give our attention? He did not; but he made sure that he left our brothers holding the mirror so that we would continue looking at his reflection. Now we should be looking at ourselves and not be trying to shift blame on to somebody who is no longer here. I have heard about you all from other people on this side. Our people on the other side don't know you any longer—they don't know us, and we are blood brothers, same flesh and bone. In fact I am so far back in time I must hope to be known, not to talk of being remembered. (*He gets up.*) You are Mammy Yoko. I have heard about you. I met you before, but I did not know that you are Bai Bureh. Sir Milton, you are prominent enough on the other side. They talk about you sometimes. Ebenezer Calendar, your music used to be everywhere, but I don't know what they are doing with it now. Well!—Who has not heard about the man from Wilberforce with a bust in front of the City Hall? Akunna Wallace-Johnson. You know, I was at the Ministry of Information a few years back and I could not get a single line about you? I was looking to see your one-time friend, but it may be he decided to stay away from these parts. His grandfather changed my destiny. When I look at you all, I see and feel a sense of commitment and integrity which is woefully foreign to our people today.

BAI BUREH: You are a very persuasive speaker. Let us know you at least by name before you tell us more about our people.

SENGBE: I am Sengbe Pieh from Mani.

BAI BUREH: Some people think I am a great fighter, but I want everybody to take a look at one of our greatest fighters and emancipators. (*They embrace.*) It is a pleasure to meet you.

AKUNNA: Most of our battles were on home soil—familiar terrain; but you had to contend with forces alien to your nature. I am certainly honoured to enjoy this privilege. (*They embrace.*)

SIR MILTON: Sengbe Pieh, as first Prime Minister of our beloved nation I am highly honoured to make your acquaintance, and to decorate you with the Order of Sierra Leone and invest you with the freedom

The Broken Handcuff

of Sierra Leonean minds, hearts and lips. In the late 1950s, I endeavoured to get our cultural heritage through artists, craftsmen, other performers and indigenous cultural institutions, assembled, preserved, disseminated. I am not so sure that the impetus was enough to ensure that the drive continues into the present decade. I am particularly worried because of what you have just told us, but I will ask Lavalie for proof. Kini Lavalie!—

SIR MILTON: Let me see the National Dance Troupe in action.

LAVALIE: Let the drums of the Lion Mountains come out! (*The drums sound.*) Let the drummers, singers and dancers show their national blend of rhythm and cultural fire! (*No response.*)

SIR MILTON: Lavalie, where is the National Dance Troupe?

LAVALIE: They live in Aberdeen Village, Sir.

SIR MILTON: I know that. You mean the Cultural Village at Aberdeen.

LAVALIE: Well, yes, Sir! But the roads are—well, not so much the roads, Sir—but there are no telephones to summon them here; their costumes are tattered and torn; their properties and instruments largely in need of repairs or replacement. They lack a means of transportation and even their meals are not as regular as before.

SIR MILTON: You mean the National Dance Troupe? What do they have then?

LAVALIE: Some of them should have ulcers, but most of them don't have the physique that will either compliment their costumes or be enhanced by the costumes, so I suggest that we leave our guest of honour to tell the story of his life. (*As the lights begin to fade they reaffirm their pledge.*)

PEOPLE: We raise up our hearts and our voices on high,
The hills and the valleys re-echo our cry,
Firmly united, ever we stand,
Singing thy praise O native land.

Blackout.

PART ONE—SCENE FOUR

LIFE IN THE VILLAGE—SUN AND MOON IN COMBAT

The stage is lit to give the effect of a reasonably bright moonlit night. The brightness is disturbed by clouds, then by a more opaque body to create the effect of an eclipse gradually taking place. The people come out with drums chanting incantations and songs to ward off the eclipse. (Possibly aided by recordings.) A sketchy and nervous dance sequence will take place, indicative of the people's anxieties. This will gradually flow into the people settling down for a storytelling session about a farmer/hunter while other traditional games are taking place. As the lighting is used to indicate dead of night with accompanying nocturnal sounds and then dawn, the people will drift away to their homes.

The Next Day—Burnah's House

Magru *is sitting on the log/stool counting potatoes in groups of four.*

MAGRU: Ta, fele, sawa, nani! *(Repeatedly.)*

Miatta *enters and they exchange fairly lengthy greetings in Mende until* Miatta *suddenly breaks into English.*

MIATTA: In fact our own rice and cocoa have not done well this year. I am afraid to think of the next rainy season.

MAGRU: For us we will have to manage the other crops like groundnuts and sell some of our ginger. The men will also try to get fish and hunt for cutting-grass[4] and wild goats as they always do.

MIATTA: But you should not worry too much. When I saw Burnah the other day he told me that your rice harvest was good. You can sell some.

MAGRU: If we don't sell we can exchange. Your hunters always get a lot of meat from animals to salt and dry; so you should—

MIATTA: Some of them went out to hunt yesterday but the moonshine let them down, so they came back empty handed.

MAGRU: I heard a lot of noise and I could not sleep easily.

The Broken Handcuff

MIATTA: It was the people; almost the entire village was out in the playground singing and beating as they tried to drive the sun away from the moon.

MAGRU: So the wrestling match took place yesterday. I wonder what would have happened if they did not beat and sing so loudly.

MIATTA: Whenever the sun and moon fight something evil happens after that. That is why I always fear these things.

MAGRU: I have more serious problems than sun and moon fights to worry about.

MIATTA: What kind of problems?

MAGRU: Are you going to stay long?

MIATTA: I don't have plenty of work to do this morning.

MAGRU: Well, please help me to pound some groundnuts as we talk. Burnah likes plenty of it in his soup—That man likes his stomach too much.

MIATTA: But he says thank you in his own way. You feed him well during the day so he looks after you very well at night.

MAGRU: He does not always wait for the night to come for him to look after me. Sometimes when he comes home from the farm he will call me "come quickly!" Thinking that it is something urgent I would rush into the room only for him to put me down on the mat. Before I know what is happening to me he is busy.

MIATTA: And you don't like that?

MAGRU: Not always—always. Sometimes after that I don't want to cook again, but just lie down and sleep. But after a short time he will ask me for his food. Sometimes if I am slow to go and prepare his food he will put me down on the mat again until he is ready to do it again. Then he will say that was for breakfast. Even this morning I was late to make the fire.

MIATTA: But you work for him so he will not say you are late for work.

MAGRU: That is what he is always saying to me. "Don't worry, we are not working for a master so we can begin when we like."

MIATTA: Magru, if I have that problem I will not worry too much. The problem I don't know how to solve is a man who will not call me even to come quickly during the day, and who will lie down looking up at the ceiling as though the farm was there, and dreaming even when he is not asleep.

MAGRU: Miatta, you will tire. Don't pray for the one I have. Sometimes I am busy doing my work or in the middle of my cooking and he will come from the farm running——

BURNAH: (*Runs in.*) Magru! (*Calls with his hand as he makes for the hut.*) Magru!

MAGRU: (*Looks helplessly at* Miatta.) Is anything wrong?

BURNAH: (*From inside.*) Come! Come quickly!

MAGRU: (*To* Miatta.) You see my trouble?

BURNAH: Magru, ask Miatta to help you with the soup, I want to talk to you quickly. (Miatta *looks on in disbelief. She picks up the pestle and begins to pound while singing.*)

MIATTA: (*Sings a little song in Mende.*) This man is strange. He is not even afraid to say "ask Miatta to help you with the soup!" But they did not send for me to come—Now that lazy hunter of mine will be lying down looking up at the ceiling and I am here feeling so funny and silly that I am here. This is why Bendu always says that it is very painful to smell or see others eating delicious food that you cannot taste. (*Pounds again as she chants.*) Smɛl nɔ tes!—Smɛl nɔ tes!

Magru *comes out adjusting her cloth, her face showing mixed feelings.* Miatta *laughs teasingly as* Burnah *comes out.*

BURNAH: Miatta, so you are helping Magru to take care of my stomach? Thank you! I will send some rice for you when the rains begin.

MIATTA: Thank you. I shall be looking for it.

MAGRU: You have said what you wanted to say to me, go and leave us to talk.

BURNAH: Are you jealous?

MAGRU: Who will be jealous for someone like you?

The Broken Handcuff

BURNAH: She always pretends she is driving me away when she really wants me to be near her. But now that I have known her she will not get me again. (*He goes.*) I am going.

MAGRU: Go!

MIATTA: Magru, I should be going. If that hunter is at home, when I get back, either he catches me or I will hunt him down. Today he will give it to me or I will take it from him.

MAGRU: But you have not told me what you came to see me for.

MIATTA: You knew before I told you. (*Going.*)

MAGRU: Truly I don't know what you——

MIATTA: You have already given me the answer. (*Goes.*)

MAGRU: (*Collecting her things.*) Oh!—Now I see what she means. So, sometimes too much of one thing is better than nothing at all. (*As she goes out* Lavalie *comes in smiling.*)

Capture

LAVALIE: That was just one slice of village life in those days. Today those who know book tell us that when a person works too much and does not play he will look like a sick man. You have seen how Burnah and Magru mixed work and play. I feel sorry for Miatta, her own man does not like to play and her head is full of thoughts. That man is a very good hunter, but he is very superstitious. They went to the bush one day—

Hunters enter.

FIRST HUNTER: Dakpe, since we have our guest with us we have to be careful. You stay at the back and let him be in the middle between us.

SECOND HUNTER: Dakpe, you know that I am always very careful even when we don't have strangers. Behind is my favourite position.

FIRST HUNTER: But you must not be too far back because when we get deeper into the forest you will have to help me watch for the animal.

SECOND HUNTER: Brima!

FIRST HUNTER: E!

SECOND HUNTER: You remember the very first time when we came into the bush with Banya?

FIRST HUNTER: Which Banya?

SECOND HUNTER: Banya who comes from Pujehun and went to Moyamba where he married Lombeh, the sister of Kona, Kona the wife of the blacksmith from Blama, whose elder brother your own younger brother beat near the barray, on the day when the dancers from Jimmi came to our place, to pay their respects to the chief, when his wife's outside sister, Bendu, Bendu the girl who you—

FIRST HUNTER: Ah! You mean Banya, my neighbour?

SECOND HUNTER: Yes!

FIRST HUNTER: Borbor.

SECOND HUNTER: I?

FIRST HUNTER: Why did you not say Banya, my neighbour at the beginning, instead of going all over the provinces?

SECOND HUNTER: You have two Banyas who are neighbours to you and the two of them are tall and black.

FIRST HUNTER: Well, is it the one that stays on my right or left?

SECOND HUNTER: No, it is not those ones. Don't you know Banya whose house is in front of your mother's house, down the road from where Kini Rogers found his wife with her boyfriend that night—

FIRST HUNTER: Well, that is the one to my right.

SECOND HUNTER: Oh! I see! I did not think so.

FIRST HUNTER: So what happened to him?

SECOND HUNTER: Dakpe, you want to tell me you have forgotten about Banya?

FIRST HUNTER: I know Banya, but I don't know what you are trying to tell me about Banya.

The Broken Handcuff

SECOND HUNTER: You remember when he was the last man in the line of hunters and he was watching for the animal and when the animal came out of the bush behind him he stood looking at it until he fainted?

FIRST HUNTER: I remember that day.

LAVALIE: Did you kill the animal?

SECOND HUNTER: Who me?

LAVALIE: Yes!

SECOND HUNTER: The whole village knows that I don't like killing but I like the beef. That is why they insist that I must always come so that I can warn the others when the animal appears.

LAVALIE: Why don't you just stay at home?

FIRST HUNTER: Dakpe, let us keep quiet. I can hear sound in the bush. If the animal hears us it will not come.

SECOND HUNTER: Dakpe, where is the dog?

FIRST HUNTER: It is with Kakpindi.

SECOND HUNTER: I think this is the time to spread out. Hold your cutlass ready. Dakpe, keep your eye open!

FIRST HUNTER Borbor!

SECOND HUNTER: E!

FIRST HUNTER: Keep quiet! Go to the right by that big tree. (*To* Lavalie.) You watch the area near that tree. I will take the area around here. My mind keeps going back to the sun and moon fight and their refusal to give us light.

SECOND HUNTER: Think about the animal that will come.

FIRST HUNTER: I am worried.

SECOND HUNTER: Why?

FIRST HUNTER: Something is going to happen.

SECOND HUNTER: Yes! We will soon catch the animal.

FIRST HUNTER: It is not that.

SECOND HUNTER: Are you afraid your wife will run away?

LAVALIE: (*Excitedly.*) Ta wama o! Ta wama!

FIRST HUNTER: Wu toa?

SECOND HUNTER: E—nyea jia?

LAVALIE: Ta wama!

SECOND HUNTER: O tas?

FIRST HUNTER: Nko—koei!

LAVALIE: Ngelei loi! Ngelei loi!

FIRST HUNTER: O taa?

SECOND HUNTER: Dakpe, we lei ma, lo-mpa da o! Lo-mpa da!

LAVALIE: Ta wama! Ta wama! Ta wama!

FIRST HUNTER: Huoh-huoh!

SECOND HUNTER: Wu toa?

FIRST HUNTER: O taa?

LAVALIE: Ta wama!

FIRST HUNTER: Ngeliei loi!

LAVALIE: Ta wama!

SECOND HUNTER: Lo-mpa da!

LAVALIE: Ta wama!

SECOND HUNTER: O taa?

LAVALIE: Ta wama!

FIRST HUNTER: Dakpe, o taa?

LAVALIE: Ta wama!

SECOND HUNTER: Shhh—!

FIRST HUNTER: (*Whispering.*) Wu toa?

The Broken Handcuff

SECOND HUNTER: No! But I see something else.

LAVALIE: (*Rising as* Two Natives *enter with rope and cutlasses in their hands.*) The superstitious hunter finally has reason to justify his fear. Disappearances of young men and women on the way to the stream, marketplace or farm were common.

FIRST NATIVE: He always comes this way.

SECOND NATIVE: Are you sure he will come today?

FIRST NATIVE: He goes to his farm every day.

SECOND NATIVE: If he is sick today?

FIRST NATIVE: Then you will take his place.

SECOND NATIVE: A! Dakpe, he will surely come.

FIRST NATIVE: Get the rope ready and stop talking.

SECOND NATIVE: I feel afraid when I keep quiet.

FIRST NATIVE: We cannot go back now.

SECOND NATIVE: That man is very strong.

FIRST NATIVE: How do you know?

SECOND NATIVE: Dakpe, he is tall? Do you see his shoulders?

FIRST NATIVE: If you are so scared of him you will go to sleep before the man comes. Then what will happen to me?

SECOND NATIVE: Are you afraid?

FIRST NATIVE: When you talk too much.

SECOND NATIVE: The rope is ready, let us practice what we will do when he comes, because we must not make mistakes.

FIRST NATIVE: We must not be too ready.

SECOND NATIVE: Lo-mpa da!

FIRST NATIVE: (*Grabs* Second Native.) Wu toa?

SECOND NATIVE: No, but we must be ready.

FIRST NATIVE: Dakpe, ta wama. (Sengbe *enters*.)

SECOND NATIVE: Are you ready?

FIRST NATIVE: Let us go back.

SECOND NATIVE: I shall shout and tell him you are here.

FIRST NATIVE: I am ready.

> Sengbe *puts his cutlass on the ground and removes his shoulder bag. He takes out a piece of cassava and begins to eat while humming in a crouching position, engrossed while the* Natives *stealthily approach. Too late to get his cutlass, they are on him. A dance sequence of capture follows. Overpowered, he is tied up, his right arm to his neck. As they take him out* Lavalie *comes out of hiding.*

LAVALIE: Today is a bad day for hunting. I wonder if it has anything to do with the sun and the moon fighting the other night.

FIRST HUNTER: I believe so. I am always scared when they fight. Sometimes I don't fear very much for myself but for my friends and their children.

LAVALIE: Why?

FIRST HUNTER: Many of my friends have been lost during hunting trips. Many of them have lost children. We have made sacrifices, but sometimes it looks like the sacrifices cause more children to disappear.

SECOND HUNTER: Last year during harvest two of our friends who came with us to hunt went home and never saw their wives again. One of them was taken with her two children.

FIRST HUNTER: I was lucky one of my friends told me to send my children away.

LAVALIE: Did he know something was going to happen?

FIRST HUNTER: I don't know but he is a friend I trust and he does many things for me. If I am tired because I don't sleep very well during the night and I cannot go to the farm, he will help me with food.

SECOND HUNTER: That is why Miatta is always vexed with you. She says you are always in bed looking up at the ceiling. Sometimes she does

The Broken Handcuff

not know when you go out hunting. She does not even know the friends you go hunting with.

FIRST HUNTER: When I lie down on my bed looking up something always happens. I always do that when I want to think.

SECOND HUNTER: Are you thinking now?

LAVALIE: I think we must go back and tell the chief and the village what has happened.

SECOND HUNTER: But the chief will ask what we did as hunters when we saw the men attack his son.

FIRST HUNTER: We will tell him that they were too many and that when we tried to help him they seized our cutlasses.

SECOND HUNTER: Why did they not kill us or take us along with his son? The chief is not stupid, he will ask many questions. I am afraid.

FIRST HUNTER: Shh! I think some more men are coming this way. If they attack us let us surrender and wait until they take us to their own place and then plan to escape. Let us hope that I know one or two of them.

LAVALIE: I don't think I will know anyone of them and it will be easy for them to buy me from you.

FIRST HUNTER: What are you talking about?

LAVALIE: Borbor, let us go.

SECOND HUNTER: But you don't know the way.

LAVALIE: It is better to get lost in the bush and be alive than to have company which will lead you into captivity with your eyes open.

SECOND HUNTER: Do you think Brima will sell us?

LAVALIE: I can feel it in my heart and bones. I believe he knows about many people who have disappeared. Borbor, let us go before it is too late (*He runs out.*)

FIRST HUNTER: The man is old and crazy.

SECOND HUNTER: Brima, is it true?

FIRST HUNTER: Do you want to leave me and go with him?

SECOND HUNTER: Is it true?

FIRST HUNTER: You are my friend I will not do such a thing.

SECOND HUNTER: Is it true that you have done it before?

FIRST HUNTER: You are afraid because of that old man?

SECOND HUNTER: Did you know about Kalilu?

FIRST HUNTER: Let the old man go and meet his doom.

SECOND HUNTER: Did you know about my sister?

FIRST HUNTER: I wanted your sister but she said no.

SECOND HUNTER: And you sold a woman you love?

FIRST HUNTER: She hurt me, and I did not want to lose two ways.

SECOND HUNTER: So Lavalie was right, you knew.

FIRST HUNTER: I can't bring her back.

SECOND HUNTER: You will pay for this, Brima.

FIRST HUNTER: I will give Miatta to you.

SECOND HUNTER: You are a devil.

FIRST HUNTER: Just give me one last chance.

SECOND HUNTER: I will tell all this to the Chief.

FIRST HUNTER: It is too late.

SECOND HUNTER: You try to stop me.

FIRST HUNTER: I will not.

SECOND HUNTER: The whole village will know.

FIRST HUNTER: They will, but not from you, because you will not get away. You should have left with Lavalie. He is a wise old man. He may lose his way and be found, you could have shown him the way, but you have just lost your freedom. You waited for too long. I come from a stock that can make others wait.

The Broken Handcuff

He begins to laugh as Borbor *is captured. Payment is handed over to him.*

First Hunter: I cannot go back to my village, everyone will soon know what I have been doing.

First Native: Then you will also have to come with us to the man, Mayagilalo. We must not make mistakes. He will decide what happens to you.

First Hunter: Find another village for me.

Second Native: First, let me hold the money bag for you.

First Hunter: Thank you. Which village will I go to?

First Native: The boat that goes out to the big seas tomorrow will make a good village for you.

Second Native: This is your friend?

First Hunter: Yes he is my friend.

Second Hunter: It will not be good to part you. You will go together.

The two are chained together.

End of Part One

PART TWO — SCENE ONE

IN TRANSIT FROM LOMBOKO

The lights meet Sengbe *sitting at the centre stage with* Lavalie *passing through downstage.*

Lavalie: Sengbe Pieh was given the opportunity to speak in public even while learning to speak the language of his hosts in the United States. Thanks to the Abolitionists.

Sengbe: Me, about 1813, in home town Mani, Sengbe Pieh, me I was born. Papa, my own, you, chief for Mani. New Year 1839, I got to farm, on road, man-man-man-man (*simulates fighting*) come from bush quick, and fight, me tie, hand to neck. Take me to go, not free no more. Mr. Sengbe Pieh, I think, no more not free. To Fule—village, I go wait. Mayagilalo he keep me. (*Counts to three while miming day and night.*) Then Mayagilalo I leave go to Siaka—Mana Siaka his town one month I stay. Stay one month Siaka, then march. Me go Lomboko. Not free!

LAVALIE: It is true. All that he has said. He was also married with two girls and a boy. In Lomboko he was kept prisoner with many other captives, predominantly Mendes from the surrounding area, as they waited to be transported across the Atlantic. Lomboko was a notorious slave trading island close to Sulima on the Gallinas coast. At Lomboko he was sold to the richest slave master. He will show you what happened. (*The others begin to come in one by one as Sengbe talks before they sing.*)

SENGBE: I was made to forfeit my natural liberty. A man called Franklin calls it an atrocious debasement of human nature. Yes, that is what slavery is. To tell you and show you all the details of how I was sold, how my countrymen were sold into slavery? It will be like going through the experience all over again. It was degrading, insulting, inhumanly degrading, humiliating, disgraceful. To think of it again makes me want to cry and to kill those who did it. Please don't humiliate me any more by asking me to go through it all again. It is not a sport, it is not pleasant. Just imagine the worst situation you think a man can be subjected to in terms of losing his freedom. I know you have powerfully creative minds. That's where it all started—in the human mind. Take some of the torture off my mind and I will show you just a little bit.

SLAVES: In the *Teçora*!
    In the *Teçora*!
       In the *Teçora*!
    From Lomboko! From Lomboko!
    Inside the *Teçora*—ra
    We were bundled like pigs—
    (*Spoken.*) —————CRAMPED!

The Broken Handcuff

All toge——ther.
Bound for Havana in Cuba
We lost sight of sunshine and air—
   They were taken from us
We lost our freedom—
We had nothing.
No father!
   No mother!
      No brother!
         No sister!
            No wife or child!
         No family!
(*To rowing movements.*) From the continent of Africa—
   We crossed the great Atlantic!
The Atlantic behind our backs
   We landed in Havana (*Disembark.*)
In Havana we left *Teçora*—
   And acquired the *Amistad*
To take us—
   To Puerto Principe—
      Puerto Principe in three days!

But our hearts said no!
And the winds said No!
To and fro—
Up and down—
North and South—
East and West—
Left and Right—
All over the sea.

LAVALIE: This backward and forward movement started in March and they arrived at Havana in June. From what my short experience of estrangement from family and friends taught me, I can tell you on their behalf without doubt, that it was not a pleasant experience.

SLAVES: In Havana!
 In Havana! (*Bells as in auction.*)
 The bells started ringing
 The bells continued ringing
 The bells stopped ringing
 A Spanish man—he came
 He bought me!
 He bought him!
 He bought me!
 He bought her!
 He bought me!
 He bought him!
 He bought you!
 He bought us!
 Forty-nine he bought.
 Another Spanish man—he came
 He bought!
 He bought!
 Three boys and a girl he bought.

BURNAH: June 26, fifty-three people, me one of them, we all like pigs squeezed into the *Amistad*. They ship was friendship. Spanish man he buy. Then ship not friendship no more, but *Amistad*. The man who get the ship Ramon Ferrer. He be captain. He drive ship.

GRABO: For we big strong and health, Spanich man he pay $450 for everyone. Fifty-three, all African people. The ship, it get ship master, ship men, Antonio-cabin boy; Celestino-cook; and two white shipmen.

BURNAH: On ship, dishes, cloth, jewelry and plenty of things.

SENGBE: They say we go to Puerto Principe. (*Falls into a formation indicative of relief from congestion and discomfort. Two white men enter talking.*)

WHITEMAN: Vat is ze veza like for sailing?

SAILOR: Look like goot. To Puerto Principe, normal veza; sri days. I sake sri days—Goot? You like? Sri days arrive.

WHITEMAN: Vel vat vil you do after vi arrive? (*Observes slaves looking. Pounces on them with whip.*) I bring up zem on zek for fresh air, sunlight; but ze look like eat me. So I put zem zown again.

The Broken Handcuff

SAILOR: Zis peoples, animals. No srit like humans. Do zat, mistake. Give zem food and ven ze arrive vok hard—Goot?

WHITEMAN: Goot. (*Drives slaves off.*) Me lie zown.

Lights used to give the impression of days and nights passing by.

PART TWO—SCENE TWO

THE MUTINY

Three days later. Lights come on with Whitemen *already on one side of the stage.*

WHITEMAN: Vi look like far from land and zis is sri days on zi sea. Vat vi do now?

SAILOR: Vat vi do? Nor! (*Angry.*) Vat I do? You not sail, I sail. I fight ze vind, ze boat fight ze vind, you not fight ze vind. Not easy, not easy; hard to fight ze vind. Ze vind sake vorta (*gestures to indicate waves*) and make big vaves. Big vaves on ship. Vat I do? I do norsin. I vate. (*They pace the deck angrily for some time and as the lights fade they go off giving way to the* Slaves. *The lights come up again.*)

BURNAH: (*Looks up.*) Why? Whiteman make too much noise today. He shout at other whiteman. But they not fight.

SENGBE: The whitemen are not very happy because the weather is bad for sailing. The storm is now three days and we are very far from land.

SLAVES: We go this way!
We go this way!
To and fro—
Up and down—
North and south—
East and West—
Left and Right—
All over the sea.

SENGBE: The storm is rough, and they have to fight the heat and the rain. Ramon Ferrer has taken his mattress on to the deck but he cannot sleep.

GRABO: Because the ship not go where they want to go, they not go to shore. But that their business. But me, to eat one banana, two potatoes and small water in small cup the whole day? This hard, too hard. I not like it.

SENGBE: You don't like it do something to show that you will not continue to accept it.

GRABO: What I do?

BURNAH: I am wanting to drinking more water.

GRABO: You to wait tomorrow.

BURNAH: No! I not wait more. Inside I dry. (*He goes for the water and is caught. Ruiz flogs him. There is an uneasy calm.*)

SENGBE: That is not right. Why a man must think he is better than another man? Because he white? Because he big? Because he tall? I tall too! I big too! He eats food, I eat too! He drinks water, I drink too! When the food and the water come out down there, it is not nice. My own not nice too. So why he better than I am?—How he better than I am? How he better than me? (Celestino *enters, motions towards a barrel of beef, and gestures with his hand across his neck, laughing as he goes.*) So!—So! (*Rubbing his hands for some time.*) So they are going to kill me; kill Burnah; kill Grabo; kill all of us to make food for others. Sometime the meat we eat come from other people like us. So we too become meat for others. No! It is a lie. It will not happen. (*Excitedly.*) It is a lie! (*The others jump and he calms them.*)

GRABO: What happen?

SENGBE: Nothing!

GRABO: Why you shout so, if nothing happen?

SENGBE: Because I want something to happen. To happen to you; to me; to Burnah; to every one of us. Something good.

GRABO: So you shout?

SENGBE: Grabo! (*Taking him aside.*) You are a father like me. Our children are not here. They will never see us again if we just sit down, waiting and staring at each other. We may see them if we fight to be free. If

The Broken Handcuff

we fail, that will not be important. But it will be good for us to try for freedom. I don't want to go alone and leave all the others. No? If I go and die for my freedom, even if my children don't see me again I will feel good in my spirit. Grabo, do you want to die like a slave?

GRABO: I not die like slave.

SENGBE: Then we must fight for freedom.

GRABO: I ready to fight.

SENGBE: Let us sit down. (*He sees a huge nail on the floor.*) This will be good to have as a friend in the time of fight——(*Looks at it and keeps it.*) Grabo, you saw what they did to Burnah? Burnah is a big man. At home in Mani, Burnah will tell his child go give me a cup of water—a calabash of palm wine—a plate of rice! Now Burnah must take a cup of water for a whole day. If we make them do this to all of our people we will die one after the other. We must stop it.

GRABO: I ready to help you stop it.

SENGBE: This is what we shall do.

WHITEMAN: (*Enters angrily.*) Vat is zis? Why you not sitting vit ze orzers? You sink you ar special? You sink you are bigmen? You big special. You norsing. You slave! You not bigmen. You big black slave. (*Pointing at Sengbe's head.*) Get up. Go sit zoen vit ze orzers.

SAILOR: (*Entering.*) Vat is ze matter?

WHITEMAN: Zits two men, ze zont vant to sit zown vit ze orzers. Ze vant make trouble.

SAILOR: Ze need more fresh air? No!

WHITEMAN: Alright! Go zown again. All of you go zown again. (*They go.*)

SAILOR: But you like be very careful so zat ze zont be very sick or du somesin serible.

WHITEMAN: Somesime I sink zat if I srit zem vit soo much care ze become soo srong and fight me. But if I vip zem soo much ze lose vet; ze lose value. So now I sleep and vake up in ze morning near ze land? I sell zem and make money. (*Laughs heartily.*)

There is a period of intense quiet which is suddenly broken by the attack of the Captives as they mutiny. Sounds of anguish, choking and terror fill the air as they dance out the attack. Lighting could go with strobe effect to accentuate the pace and horror. A few deaths.

PART TWO—SCENE THREE

THE TRIALS (*MANI INSET*)

An Abolitionist *enters with a billboard and a bell against the background of the court room upstage.* Judge *seated in a freeze up centre, billboard at down stage.*

ABOLITIONIST: To you lovers of freedom, I crave your support for a worthy cause. Thirty-eight Africans inhumanly bundled from their native land and made to endure atrocious cruelties across seas are now locked up in jail awaiting trial for crimes they are alleged to have committed. They lack knowledge of the practices of civilized society, our language and the obligations of Christianity. The plight of these unfortunate men demand our attention, and several friends of human rights have held consultation upon the case of these Africans and decided to appoint a committee to employ interpreters and three competent and distinguished legal gentlemen and to undertake any necessary expenses to secure their rights. We therefore appeal to you lovers of freedom, liberty, humanity, to help meet the needs of our friends through generous donations which can be sent to the above mentioned who will acknowledge your gifts and surrender a public account of all their disbursement. (*He exits as* Judge Smith Thompson *concludes the first trial.*)

SMITH THOMPSON: I therefore refuse the writ of habeas corpus for the release of these girls. I must also state that this circuit court lacks jurisdiction to determine crimes of murder and piracy, where the same were committed on a Spanish ship and in Spanish waters. Furthermore, property claims not excluding those of Ruiz and Montez to these natives should be decided in a District Court. (*He exits as* Lavalie *enters with a bucket which he deposits at the centre stage.*)

The Broken Handcuff

LAVALIE: The captives were returned to jail to await another trial. (*Sengbe enters in a pensive mood.*) While they waited their abolitionist friends got busy. Naturally the pressure was on all of them. (*Indicates Sengbe.*) His mind is full. These are the very cold days which compel you to think warm thoughts. (*The others come in severally with cups.*).

WOMAN: You dance because you not want use money. You fear to be poor?

BURNAH: My people, they far far from me, so . . .

GRABO: We all same—people all far far from we . . .

SENGBE: So let us do something now, so that not long we go back to them. We don't cry for them every day. They don't cry for us every day. You . . . big man! You . . . big woman! Mende people strong! Let us think to help our friends get us back to Mende people. (*Pause. The District Court. Lights momentarily on* Judson *as he prepares to give his verdict.*) . . . . We come from Mende land. We not ladinos, not Spanish; Spanish he lie. We not happy, but we laugh to keep our lives. Colonel Pendelton say white people fear us too much when we not smile and tell us we will die if we make white people afraid. We love peace, we love people. Colonel Pendelton he put us in chains; he ship our bodies; they hurt all over with pain. Why? We not animals; we not slaves; we people like white people; but we come from another place. We love peace; we love life; we love freedom—Give us free . . . give us free . . . . . (*Two women get him to sit down.*)

JUDGE JUDSON: This is my judgement dated this 13th day of January in the year 1840, delivered in this Hartford District Court of Connecticut in the United States of America. I do declare that in violation of Spanish law the Amistad captives had been kidnapped and sold into slavery. As they were legally free men I therefore order that they be transported back to Africa from where they had been taken against their will. (*Two* Men *leap up and begin a harvest/freedom dance. The others join in singing for a brief while. Then they freeze.* John Quincy Adams *appears upstage agonizing over his decision to accept being a Defence Counsel. The pressure and apprehension are evident on the now sombre faces of the* Captives.)

ADAMS: The devil and his host stand against any man on American soil who shall think of putting an end to the African Slave Trade. And as I approach my 74th birthday with drowsy faculties how can I honour my God and mankind and be instrumental in achieving human emancipation and the eradication of the African slave trade? How can I? . . . But my conscience gives me no rest. Let me but die upon breach. (*Pacing up and down for a while.*) Oh, how shall I do justice to this case and to these men? (*Enter Attendant with an envelope for Adams. Cuts it open. Voice of letter is mechanised.*)

VOICE: Dear Friend Mr Adams, I want to write a letter to you because you love Mendi people and you talk to the grand court. We want to tell you one thing. Jose Ruiz say we born in Havana, he tell lie . . . we all born in Mendi.

We want you to ask the court what we have done wrong? What for Americans keep us in prison? Some people say Mendi people crazy; Mendi people dolt; because we no talk American language. Merica people no talk Mendi language; Merica people dolt?

They tell bad things about Mendi people and we no understand. Some men say Mendi people very happy because they laugh and have plenty to eat. Mr Pendelton come and Mendi people all look sorry because they think about Mendi land and friends we no see now. Mr Pendelton says Mendi people no look sorry again—that why we laugh. But Mendi people feel sorry; O, we cant tell how sorry. Some people say Mendi people no have souls. Why we feel bad, if we no have souls?

Dear Friend Mr Adams you have children, you have friends, you love them; you feel sorry if Mendi people come and carry them all to Africa. We feel bad for our friends, and our friends all feel bad for us—

If American people give us free we glad, if they no give us free we sorry—we sorry for Mendi people little, we sorry for American people great deal, because God punish liars. We want you to tell court that Mendi people no want to go back to Havana, we no want to be killed. Dear friend, we want you to know how we feel. Mendi people think, think, think. Nobody know what we think; the

The Broken Handcuff

                teacher he know, we tell him some. Mendi people have got souls—
                All we want is to make us free.

SENGBE: Brea . . . k these chains
                And set me free
                And let me go

                O give we free!

OTHERS: Give we free!

SENGBE: O give we free!

OTHERS: Give we free!

SENGBE: O whiteman—
                Give . . . me free and let me go
                You took me out from me people
                And you make me a slave ...
                I fought and broke my chains
                So let me go.

OTHERS: Let him go!
                (*Pointing at each other as they sing.*)
                O give him free!
                    Give him free!
                O give him free!
                    Give him free!
                O whiteman
                Give . . . him free and let him go
                You took him out from him people
                And you make him slave
                He fought he broke him chains . . .
                So let him go!
        (*Defiantly.*)   O give we free!
                    Give we free!
                O give we free!
                    Give we free!
                O whiteman—
                Give . . . we free and make we go
                You take we out from we people

> And you make we slaves
> We fight—we broke we chains
> So give we free!
>
> Give we free!
>
> So give we free!
> Give we free ....!

The judges are represented by nameplates. As the nameplates are positioned and the song dies down the actors also resume their position for the court.

ADAMS: (*In progress.*) The rights of my clients to their lives and liberties having been so thoroughly defended by my distinguished colleague, I can only say that I am consoled by the thought that his court is a court of Justice.

In any litigation between two parties justice demands that each enjoys protection by the court. Of crucial importance this is, because I represent thirty-six persons whose continued existence and liberty rest with the decision of the court.

I am compelled to declare myself consoled by the fact that I am before a court of justice because as I shall show, another arm of government has adopted a stance of utter injustice, and my clients await their fate from its decision, under the weight of the combined executive powers of two nations.

Press not a falling man too far. (*Turns in the direction of the prosecution.*) Should I ignore the course it has pursued, even the court might conclude that the Executive was in order and that the parties I represent had not been wronged. Making this charge in defence of my clients' rights, I now examine correspondence between the Secretary of State and the Ambassador of Her Majesty, the Queen of Spain as officially communicated to Congress.

The Executive, with reference to this case has consciously displayed sympathy for the white and antipathy for the black. Nearly the entire nation now breeds that same spirit of sympathy and antipathy.

The Broken Handcuff

I do not know of any law . . . statute or constitution, no treaty applicable to the proceedings of the Executive of the Judiciary except that law (*points to a copy of the Declaration of Independence hanging against one of the pillars of the Court Room*) two copies of which continuously serve the eyes of your Honors. Except for the law of nature and of nature's God on which our fathers founded our own national existence, I am ignorant of any other that reaches the case of my clients. I trust that in its application to my clients that will be the law on which this case is decided.

My entire argument that the appeal should be thrown out is based on the assertion that the proceedings of the United States have been unjust from the onset. The seizure of the vessel and these men is wrong in the first place. The use of force to secure their arrest on New York soil was also wrong. (Adams *in freeze, the lights focus on* Lavalie *as he enters.*)

LAVALIE: That was Wednesday. Adams could not continue his defence until after a recess for Justice Barbour's death, one of the Judges dreaded by the friends of the Africans. So when Monday came for Adams to continue (*laughing as he exits*) the Negros had removed one obstacle. (*Lights return to* Adams.)

ADAMS: My name, your Honors, was entered over thirty-seven years ago on the 7th of February 1804, on both the rolls as one of the Attorneys and Counselors of this Court . . . I appear, I hope, for the last time before this Court in the cause of justice, of liberty and now of life in respect of my fellow men. Alas! Where is one of the very judges of the court in whose presence I commenced this anxious argument? Where is he? Gone! (*Pause.*) I sincerely hope and pray that he has gone to receive the rewards of heaven. As I make my exit from this Bar and Honorable Court, I can only direct a heartfelt prayer to heaven that every member . . . every one (*turns to look at the judges*) at the end of a long and virtuous career in this world, will be met with this greeting at the threshold of the next: "Well done, good and faithful servant; enter thou into the joy of the Lord." (*Bows to judges and audience. Exits.*)

LAVALIE: Adams was back on the morning of March 9. The Court room was far from full. Judge Taney got up . . . no it was Justice Story, he got up and read the verdict. Memorable words in the story of human justice. The decisions of the District and Circuit Courts were upheld. The Circuit Court was directed to order the immediate discharge of the Africans from the custody of the United States Marshal. In humility Adams heard the verdict and bowed out in thanksgiving. Down South, men were still being subjected to the atrocities of slavery. But on that day, in that case, justice and humanity were victorious. With time, Justice would cease to ask the colour of a man's skin.

SENGBE: Break these chains and set me free!

ALL: And let me go!

Lights fade with song.

PART TWO—SCENE FOUR

RETURN—DISILLUSIONMENT—DEATH AND BURIAL

As Lavalie *talks, the entire scene is mimed in the background with Mende music playing at various level as necessary. On the boat to Sierra Leone. Excitedly they talk about their home shores which they will soon see again after almost three years. They see the land. Lights fade off and when it builds up again they are coming on shore with little bundles. Some discover relations.* Sengbe *learns of the destruction of his home town. Distractedly he walks off as the others drift away leaving a bare stage. The lights go down again as Pentecostal singing breaks through. In low lights* Sengbe *comes in years later, an old, helpless and broken man. He is met by the* Pastor *on the church steps. As they talk* Sengbe *drops dead. The* Pastor *cradles his head in his hand and shouts for help. Others run in.*

LAVALIE: At last they are back on home soil. Some discover relations while Sengbe learns of the destruction of his home town and walks away distractedly to find a new home. He could not quite gather the bits and pieces together again. He becomes, like some others, part of the Christian Ministry that springs up under American guidance. But indeed, a prophet is never truly respected in his own home. The

The Broken Handcuff

years rolled by, Sengbe is now an old man as he drags his broken frame to the Church steps. (*He dies.*) The son of a chief, a potential chief himself, full of authority, dignity and poise, once a man with vitality and a happy family, was reduced by circumstances, the treachery and greed of his own brothers to the status of a slave. (*The body meanwhile is being prepared for burial in very controlled actions in the background.*) His indomitable spirit refused to accept his conscription into a breed that nature and his birth did not prescribe for him. He was borne away in shackles across the high seas to the land of liberty, the natural leader of his fellow captives, to underline that they were indeed free men. A chief even in adversity. Their lives were threatened by the efforts of some not worthy of their natural claims to the human species. But the love, the determination of a few strong-willed friends of liberty sustained their resolve to regain their freedom. Captured—taken away early in the new year of 1839, they returned early in the new year of 1842. Returned to what? For him in particular (*pointing at the body*) to ignominy at the base of the pinnacle his stature commanded as a man. The heart of one of the most famous trials in American legal history. A link between two great continents. Even though the end of that life (*again indicating the body*) fell so low, Nature can be proud of his spirit.

The last post is sounded; Sengbe's tomb stands at centre stage as the lights die out.

THE END

Acknowledgments

Photocopies of the previously unpublished scripts included in this volume, arguably among the most important Sierra Leonean dramatic works from the late twentieth century, have circulated informally for years among a small circle of Sierra Leone specialists. It is a great honor to finally make all three accessible to a broad audience of teachers, students, theater companies, and lay readers. A great many people deserve thanks for helping shepherd this project to publication.

First thanks go to Charlie Haffner, Raymond de'Souza George, and the late Yulisa Amadu Maddy for creating these wonderful plays and to Charlie and Raymond for their incredible patience in seeing this project through to completion. It is no exaggeration to say that the book could not have been completed without Elvina Desouza-Omidiran and Nadia Maddy's enthusiastic representation of their fathers throughout the publication process.

Historians of African and African diaspora drama owe Ansa Akyea an enormous debt of gratitude for preserving Yulisa Amadu Maddy's script. Akyea was a student at the University of Iowa when Maddy cast him as Sengbe Pieh in 1993. That he saved his sprawling, marked-up, multiply amended printout for over twenty years and through countless moves is, to me, a miracle. The play itself turned out to be a loose, and unofficial, adaptation of the African American novelist Barbara Chase-Riboud's novel *Echo of Lions*. For Dr. Chase's gracious enthusiasm in working with me and the Maddy family to see the play published, I am deeply grateful.

A big thanks, too, to Yuliana Ramos, whose transcription and formatting assistance saved me countless hours of labor, to the West

Acknowledgments

African Research Association for earlier financial support that indirectly benefited this book, to Shirley Jennifer Lim for strategic advice on matters large and small, to Iyunolu Folayan Osagie for sharing a copy of Raymond de'Souza George's play with me twenty years ago, and to Joe Opala for so enthusiastically championing the *Amistad* rebellion history in his adopted Sierra Leonean homeland.

Lastly, I thank Laura Murphy, Ainehi Edoro, the anonymous readers, Gillian Berchowitz, Nancy Basmajian, and the entire team at Ohio University Press.

Notes

Introduction

Epigraph: Yulisa Amadu Maddy, "His Supreme Excellency's Guest at Bigyard," *Index on Censorship* 17, no. 5 (1988): 88, paraphrasing Frantz Fanon, *The Wretched of the Earth*, transl. Constance Farrington (New York: Grove Weidenfeld, 1965), 232.

1. For data on human population displacement during the war, see United Nations Development Program Evaluation Office, "Case Study: Sierra Leone," http://web.undp.org/evaluation/documents/thematic/conflict/SierraLeone.pdf. For a multidisciplinary analysis of the conflict, see Ibrahim Abdullah, ed., *Between Democracy and Terror: The Sierra Leone Civil War* (Dakar, Senegal: CODESRIA, 2004).

2. For an image of the playbill, see http://chnm.gmu.edu/courses/jackson/amistad/files/playbil.html.

3. The broad details about the history of Sierra Leonean theater here and elsewhere in the introduction are drawn from Julius Spencer, "A Historical Background to the Contemporary Theatre in Sierra Leone," *International Journal of Sierra Leone Studies* 1 (1988): 26–35 and from my interviews with the country's theater professionals.

4. The general details about Maddy's life and career listed here and later in the introduction are drawn from Eustace Palmer, "Yulisa Amadu Maddy (1936–2014)," *Research in Sierra Leone Studies: Weave* 2, no. 1 (2014): 1–3.

5. See Peter Karefa-Smart, "Theatre and Social Change," *West Africa* (May 1988): 879–80; and Kolosa Kargbo, "In Search of a Venue," *West Africa* (October 1988): 1892.

6. Joseph A. Opala mentions the arrest in an unpublished manuscript, "Bai Bureh: The Making of a National Symbol."

7. Joseph A. Opala describes Haffner's political commitments and aesthetic strategies in *"Ecstatic Renovation!": Street Art Celebrating Sierra Leone's 1992 Revolution* (Freetown: Sierra Leone Adult Education Association, 1994), 28–32.

8. Iyunolu Folayan Osagie, "Historical Memory and a New National Consciousness: The Amistad Revolt Revisited in Sierra Leone," *Massachusetts Review* 38, no. 1 (Spring 1997): 77.

Notes

9. See Iyunolu Folayan Osagie, *The Amistad Revolt: Memory, Slavery, and the Politics of Identity in the United States and Sierra Leone* (Athens: University of Georgia Press, 2000), 106–7; and Matthew J. Christensen, *Rebellious Histories: The Amistad Slave Revolt and the Cultures of Late Twentieth-Century Black Transnationalism* (Albany: SUNY Press, 2012), chapter 2.

10. Palmer, 2–3.

11. Christensen, 114–15.

Charles Haffner, *Amistad Kata-Kata*

1. *Bondo* refers here to the Sowei initiation rituals in which girls become women. The women's Sowei society, which trains the girls in the obligations and rights of adulthood, serves as a cornerstone of Mende life, social organization, and cultural reproduction. Its reference in this scene underscores the enduring authority of Mende identity and culture. The male equivalent is called *Poro*, referenced later in the play.

2. Sengbe Pieh, Bai Bureh, Madame Yoko, Manga Sewa, Kai Londo, Ndawa, I.T.A. Wallace-Johnson, Milton Margai, Siaka Stevens.

3. A *shokoto* is a long loose gown. The *ronko* hat would have been worn by members of Sierra Leone's Limba ethnic group, not Mendes like Sengbe. Haffner's choice to dress Sengbe in the hat possibly reflects his desire to make Sengbe a national rather than a regional heroic figure.

4. Spanish law distinguished *ladinos*, enslaved Africans born and domiciled in Cuba and able to speak Spanish, from *bozales*, enslaved Africans newly imported and unable to speak Spanish. Beginning in 1817, a series of treaties outlawed the import and enslavement of *bozales*, which would have included the *Amistad* mutineers. However, as the play makes clear later in the scene, a well-established system of corruption made it easy for slave owners to falsify documentation.

5. The text does not specify what song they sing, but in performance the Freetong Players typically perform Haffner's Krio-language a capella ballad "Sengbe Pieh," included in this volume.

Yulisa Amadu Maddy, The *Amistad* Revolt

1. It is likely that Maddy refers here to U.S. Marshal Norris Wilcox. However, later in the play Maddy conflates the marshal with the Amistads' jailer Colonel Stanton Pendleton, referring to Pendleton as Marshal. Combining the two characters would certainly make more manageable the already large cast.

2. The instruction in the original manuscript is incomplete. It reads "Shaking his head, looking ?" There is no additional indication of the sentiment Maddy wanted Gibbs to express.

Notes

3. The tabulae is a large drum used most frequently in Sierra Leone by Muslims for religious purposes. In Krio, spelled tabule.

4. In Maddy's original typescript, the stage instruction reads "Slow drumming accompanied by ? uninterrupted." The instruction has been revised because there is no additional evidence to indicate what should accompany the drumming or even whether Maddy included an accompaniment when he staged the play.

5. The original typescript gives this line to Kabba Sei even though he was killed on board the *Amistad*. Whether this is a mistake on Maddy's part or a narrative tactic to give voice to the dead is unclear. Given the content of the line, it seems more likely to have been a mistake, but anyone reading or staging the play should remain open to the alternative.

6. Kale's lines here are excerpted from the letter he wrote to President John Quincy Adams. Maddy intersperses the rest of the letter throughout the play. For the full text of his letter, see *Amistad Kata-Kata* in this volume.

Raymond E. D. de'Souza George, *The Broken Handcuff*

1. This passage is in the Krio language, Sierra Leone's lingua franca. A creole language like Nigerian Pidgin, Krio is primarily an oral language. In its common written form, as seen on posters, shop signs, and the like, words are typically spelled phonetically with Latin script. De'Souza George relies instead on the official Krio lexicon which employs two special characters: "ɔ", pronounced "aw" as in "cough," and the short e, "ɛ", pronounced "eh" as in "head."

2. The historical figures appearing in this scene include Governor John Clarkson (1763–1828), the first governor of the Sierra Leone Company; Bai Bureh (ca. 1840–1908), the leader of the anticolonial 1898 Rebellion; Madam Yoko (ca. 1849–1906), a Mende chief who consolidated several chiefdoms in response to British colonization; Isaac Theophilus Akuna Wallace-Johnson (1894–1965), a trade unionist and anticolonial nationalist leader who mobilized mass support for political self-rule; Ebenezer Calendar (1912–1985), a popular musician whose songs provided a running social history of the country; and Sir Milton Margai, an anticolonial nationalist leader and Sierra Leone's first prime minister.

3. Clarkson's dialogue is taken from his "Prayer for Sierra Leone," which he delivered at the end of his governorship of the Sierra Leone Company in 1793. The full text can be found at http://www.sierra-leone.org/clarksonsprayer.html.

4. "Cutting-grass" is the common Sierra Leonean name for a civet.

Suggested Reading

Abdullah, Ibrahim, ed. *Between Democracy and Terror: The Sierra Leone Civil War*. Dakar, Senegal: CODESRIA, 2004.

Abraham, Arthur. *The Amistad Revolt: An Historical Legacy of Sierra Leone and the United States*. Freetown, Sierra Leone: United States Information Service, 1987.

———. "Sengbe Pieh: A Neglected Hero?" *Journal of the Historical Society of Sierra Leone* 2, no. 2 (1978): 22–30.

Adéẹ̀kọ́, Adélékè. *The Slave's Rebellion: Literature, History, Orature*. Bloomington: Indiana University Press, 2005.

Buba, Tony, dir. *Ghosts of Amistad: In the Footsteps of the Rebels*. Filmmakers Library, 2014. DVD.

Chase-Riboud, Barbara. *Echo of Lions*. New York: William Morrow, 1989.

Christensen, Matthew J. *Rebellious Histories: The Amistad Slave Revolt and the Cultures of Late Twentieth-Century Black Transnationalism*. Albany: SUNY Press, 2012.

Conteh-Morgan, Earl, and Mac Dixon-Fyle. *Sierra Leone at the End of the Twentieth Century: History, Politics, and Society*. New York: Peter Lang, 1999.

Conteh-Morgan, John, and Tejumola Olaniyan, eds. *African Drama and Performance*. Bloomington: Indiana University Press, 2004.

Government of Sierra Leone. *Sierra Leonean Heroes: Fifty Great Men and Women Who Helped to Build Our Nation*. 2nd ed. Freetown: Government of Sierra Leone, 1988.

Jones, Howard. *Mutiny on the Amistad: The Saga of a Slave Revolt and Its Impact on American Abolition, Law, and Diplomacy*. New York: Oxford University Press, 1987.

Lawrance, Benjamin N. *Amistad's Orphans: An Atlantic Story of Children, Slavery, and Smuggling*. New Haven: Yale University Press, 2015.

Macaluso, Laura A. *Art of the Amistad and the Portrait of Cinqué*. New York: Rowman and Littlefield, 2016.

Maddy, Yulisa Amadu. "His Supreme Excellency's Guest at Bigyard." *Index on Censorship* 17, no. 5 (1988): 88–91.

———. *No Past, No Present, No Future*. Portsmouth, NH: Heinemann, 1973.

———. *Obasai and Other Plays*. London: Heinemann, 1971.

Murphy, Laura T. *Metaphor and the Slave Trade in West African Literature*. Athens: Ohio University Press, 2012.

Suggested Reading

Ojukutu-Macauley, Sylvia, and Ismail Rashid, eds. *The Paradoxes of History and Memory in Post-colonial Sierra Leone*. Lanham, MD: Lexington Books, 2013.

Opala, Joseph A. *"Ecstatic Renovation!": Street Art Celebrating Sierra Leone's 1992 Revolution*. Freetown: Sierra Leone Adult Education Association, 1994.

Osagie, Iyunolu Folayan. *The Amistad Revolt: Memory, Slavery, and the Politics of Identity in the United States and Sierra Leone*. Athens: University of Georgia Press, 2000.

Palmer, Eustace, and Abioseh Porter. *Knowledge Is More Than Mere Words: A Critical Introduction to Sierra Leonean Literature*. Trenton, NJ: Africa World Press, 2008.

Rediker, Marcus. *The Amistad Rebellion: An Atlantic Odyssey of Slavery and Freedom*. New York: Penguin, 2013.

Sale, Maggie Montesinos. *The Slumbering Volcano: American Slave Ship Revolts and the Production of Rebellious Masculinity*. Durham, NC: Duke University Press, 1997.

Spencer, Julius. "A Historical Background to the Contemporary Theatre in Sierra Leone." *International Journal of Sierra Leone Studies* 1 (1988): 26–35.

About the Authors

MATTHEW J. CHRISTENSEN is professor of literature and cultural studies at the University of Texas, Rio Grande Valley. His publications include *Rebellious Histories: The Amistad Slave Revolt and the Cultures of Late Twentieth-Century Black Transnationalism* and articles on Anglophone African detective fiction.

CHARLIE HAFFNER is the director-general of the performance troupe the Freetong (Freetown) Players, which he founded in 1985, and currently chairs the Sierra Leonean National Monuments and Relics Commission. As a playwright and traditional communicator, he has worked extensively to use drama as a tool for education and development and to advance Sierra Leone's postwar reconciliation. His most recent play is the epic historical drama *A Nation's Journey*.

THE HONORABLE REV. RAYMOND E. D. DE'SOUZA GEORGE was appointed in May 2018 as the Minister of Works and Public Assets in the Government of Sierra Leone. He was previously a senior lecturer in the Department of History and African Studies at Fourah Bay College. Active in Sierra Leonean theater for decades, he performed on stage at FESTAC '77 and founded Mount Aureol Players. His other plays include *Bobo Lef, On Trial for a Will,* and *Priscilla's Homecoming.*

YULISA AMADU "PAT" MADDY is the author of over a dozen plays, including *Yon Kon*, for BBC Radio; *Big Berrin,* for which he was jailed in Sierra Leone; two (coauthored) studies of neoimperialism in children's literature, and a novel, *No Past, No Present, No Future*. The novel and his collection *Obasai and Other Plays* were published as part of Heinemann's African Writers Series. Maddy also directed both the Sierra Leonean and Zambian national dance troupes and founded Gbakanda Afrikan Tiata. He died in 2014.